THE COMPLETE LETTER BOOK

Multisensory Activities for Teaching Sounds and Letters

by Michele Borba and Dan Ungaro

illustrated by Michele Borba and Prtreva Ungaro

Copyright © Good Apple, Inc. 1980

ISBN #0-916456-80-3

GOOD APPLE, INC.
Box 299
Carthage, IL 62321

TABLE OF CONTENTS

Dear Teacher,

THE COMPLETE BOOK OF LETTERS is a program developed to teach letters and their sounds to young readers. The activities include exposures to the various sense modalities by fusing the letter sounds to taste, smell, sight, touch. We have aimed to provide experiences which allow children to discover and interact with letter sounds in ways most likely to assure internalization.

The activities and student pages within this book can be used as a complete, sequential program. OR, you may choose activities and contracts at random to fit into your own reading program. The book is designed to provide the teacher with such flexibility.

The letter sound program includes:

1) READY-TO-USE CONTRACTS: For each sound, a reproducible series of activities, shown clearly enough that even non-readers can follow it on their own.

2) MATERIALS AND PROCEDURES FOR CONTRACTS: Clear explanations to the teacher of the methods to be used in preparing and following the contracts.

3) SUPPLEMENTARY ACTIVITIES FOR EACH SOUND: Following each letter contract, a page of suggested special activities for reinforcing that sound.

4) BACKGROUND FOR TEACHERS: A complete explanation and rationale behind the formation of such a program.

5) PARENT LETTER: A letter, ready-to-reproduce plus two other letters designed for use in gaining parent cooperation with the program.

6) FIELD TRIP ACTIVITIES: Each letter sound is accompanied by suggestions for field trips which will reinforce the learning of that sound.

7) INTERVIEW IDEAS: For each sound, ideas are supplied for interviewing persons whose occupations or titles reinforce the sound.

8) HANDWRITING CENTER AND CONTRACT: Tactile activities for practicing the formation of letters.

9) A SAMPLE LETTER LEARNING CENTER: You may wish to develop one for each letter sound.

10) PLUS: other reinforcing activities, games and record-keeping devices.

We sincerely hope that you will find this book's activities to be joyful learning experiences as your students discover the world of sounds.

Michele Borba   Dan Ungaro

THE LETTER-SOUND PROGRAM

- Parents can play a large role in helping promote your letter sound program. By keeping them informed of the letter-of-the week and activities they can be doing, they will help reinforce your curriculum. Parent meetings and newsletters are helpful.

Dear Parents,

We have been working hard at school by laying the foundation for beginning reading by learning letter sounds. You can play a most important role in this activity by showing your child objects relating to the letter sounds we have been studying. You will receive a note each week informing you as to which sounds will be covered. It is most important that you help create the experience for the letter sounds by means of an object (a cup for "c", a spoon for "s", a pan for "p", etc). Please do not show him words at this stage.

Your child will be involved in sharing experiences on _____ day. It would be well to have as one phase of this sharing be something related to the letter sounds. For instance, if he is studying the sound "b", perhaps he could share his toy bear. Help him make a simple riddle sentence for the sharing...("This is something that begins with the same sound as "butter"...you sleep with it at night, it is cuddly...etc.). The more association that the children can have with a particular learning activity, the greater will be his retention, so your help will play a most important role in his learning.

Dear Parents,

So many things have been happening these past days in our room. We're really working hard learning so many, many concepts. It's such a joy working with such a delightful group. If their enthusiasm continues to be as high as it is now, we'll be sailing through the year.

I want especially to thank you for your cooperation with the reading program. The children have been learning words through a language experience approach. In this method, the children learn to read through their own experiences. The vocabulary words are taken directly from readers. At this stage it is so important that the children feel successful and secure with their newly acquired skills. They are rightfully quite proud of their new reading ability and this is why I've tried to make you such an important part of the program.

I feel close communication between the home and school is so extremely important. Please don't hesitate to call any time to set up a conference, to have a question clarified or just to talk.

Dear Parents,

This is a special note to let you know that next week we will be studying the sound _____ as in the word_____. Please help me find things beginning with this sound for my sound sharing day.   Love,

_____

Dear_____,

Next week our class will be studying the sound ___ as in the word _____. Items we will need at our center are:

1. _____
2. _____
3. _____

Could you please send them to school with your child by Friday so I can set up next week's center? Please let me know if you have any problems. Thank you for your support. The centers are helping children learn their sounds.

A Reading Mystery?

The great mystery of beginning reading has apparently not been solved as yet. This is evidenced by the million dropouts a year we have had for the past decade. It has been found that 90 percent of these dropouts are poor readers, so the answer to the problem seems to be as difficult to find as is the Holy Grail. However, in the opinion of many experts, the problems of beginning reading instruction have been greatly overdramatized. In their opinion all that is needed is efficient instruction which is adjusted to individual subskill needs. The nonreader is a child who has been inadequately served in the classroom, in the opinion of Dr. Durrell. He is considered to be one of our foremost experts in the field of letter sound knowledge. He has concluded that auditory perception is the most important, yet more seriously neglected, subskill in beginning reading. Durrell thinks that parents and kindergarten teachers should instruct children in letter names and sounds. This book has been written to provide guides in this area.

Speech to Print

In 1967 the U.S. Office of Education First Grade Studies were conducted. These studies of twenty-seven procedures involved thousands of first grade children. They found that the best single predictor of first grade success in reading was a letter sound program. It must be remembered that the auditory factor is not only the most important but also the most seriously neglected subskill in beginning reading. The primary symbolic language is speech, and from this we transfer to print. It is important to note that effective phonics moves **forward** from sound to print not **backward** from print to sound. In all too many schools children are launched into reading by learning sets of phonic rules (print) before learning sounds. This is backward and results in a great deal of first grade failure.

A Test

The simplest test to illustrate this point is to provide the nonreader, who has been drilled in phonic rules, sight words, and letter names by rote learning, with four letters on cards - say h, b, w and m. The child will be able to hold up the letter you name, and he will also hold up the right letter for the sounds given. But he will not know what to hold up when you ask for the first letter in house or hat, bread or bat, wagon or watch, machine or match. The same problem will exist if you ask for the last letter in the words. This problem can be overcome readily by suitable ear training, utilizing an imagineering approach.

A Good Ear For Sounds

A good ear for sounds is particularly important in learning to read a language which has 40 sound phonemes for 26 letters. If a child's ear is good, it does not stress her to discover that the "air" sound is spelled differently in chair, their, where, or bear. A good ear for sounds will result if a variety of sense exposures is provided for the young beginner. The child cannot begin to understand the operation of decoding and encoding until the phoneme unit has acquired concrete reality through her actions upon it. When a child first comes to school a "word" is simply a hunk of utterance. The first stage of comprehension, for children, of what a word, a letter or a sound is will not be grasped until a brief explanation of these tools for reading are explained. This should be provided at mid-year of kindergarten when letter sounds should be introduced. Prior to this time, the child should be exposed to a variety of sounds. These will be found in poetry, Mother Goose, and in fairy tales. He will hear loud sounds, dull sounds, sounds that cut, sounds that tear, sounds that taste, sounds that smell, sounds that glitter. Later, when he is involved in the procedures of reading, a detailed story of reading should be provided. The authors, in the companion book to this one, *Imagineering the Reading Process*, have provided such a story.

Synesthesia

Synesthesia is a fantastic and fascinating experience that has attracted the attention of poets, writers and scientists. Some have written that they have heard the clamor of colors. Koestler (*The Act of Creation*) said he could never look at a western picture without smelling the dust cloud raised by the galloping horses. Torrance promotes the process of elaboration to enhance thinking. It is a process which "listens for smells." To the 19th century poet, Rimbaud, the vowel sounds were endowed with colors. In *"Sonnet of Vowels,"* he described the A as being black, E as white, I as red, O as blue, and U as green. Our standard color code for stop-go is red and green. We speak of bright and dark sounds as well as bright and dark colors.

Enriching Memory

Sensory qualities endow memory with richness and vibrance. "Nothing awakes a reminiscence like an odor" according to Victor Hugo. *The Gingerbread Boy* will arouse many delicious odors for children, but more important they will have images created which will echo back the various sounds of letters. The feedback from these various sense blendings is truly the "via regia," the main avenue to understanding. They provide an echolocation process from the images which helps to solidify letter sound knowledge.

Internalizing Letter Sounds

Rote learning of the letter names is a useless activity. Considerable research, specifically that of Ebbinghaus, reveals that children forget 60 percent of what they have learned (of nonsense material) in the first hour. "Often we must get away from speech in order to think clearly", according to Wordsworth. When Alice in Wonderland was admonished to think carefully before speaking, she exclaimed, "How can I know what I think till I see what I say?" What both Wordsworth and Alice are alluding to is that there is a need for a thorough knowledge of things before they can be internalized to provide an automatic reaction. It is not until letter sounds are internalized that the child will have a good ear for sounds. Once we have invested the letter sound with meaning, the meaning cannot be torn from it.

Echolocation!

In order to provide an internalization of letter sounds it is necessary not only to create a sonar system of echolocation, but also it is necessary to bring into play what Bruner calls, a "combinatorial activity." Such an activity will utilize **all** of the sense modalities to enrich letter sounds. When this has been achieved, the child will be receiving a feedback from images that provide an echo of the applicable sound.

Gaining Time

A conscientious teacher, after reviewing the works of Rosseau, might be startled to come across the following notation: "The training of children is a profession where we must know how to lose time in order to gain it". Many teachers might say we have much too much to do in school as it is without being asked to lose time. However, if we reflect about what Rosseau said, we will find that it makes sense. If we are to have an echo of the correct sound we must lose time from the procedures of learning letter sounds by rote. There is a need to lose time constructively until the child has internalized things. There is an old saying that goes, "If a little bit is good, a lot is better." We might say that learned material has to "set," just as cement does. When the centipede was asked in which precise order he moved his hundred legs, he became paralyzed, and starved to death, because he never thought of it before, and had left the legs to look after themselves. Children share a similar fate when they are asked to think of a rule that provides the basis for a letter sound. They will be able to give the rule, but it will take some doing to apply it if it has not been internalized. In language, if you have to stop to think, it is too late!

A Sonar Sound System

There has been a tendency to sanitize words and letters, to wring them dry of their visual, emotional and tactile qualities. A cross blending of the senses will greatly enrich memory. Children need to develop something of a sonar system that enables them to discriminate between sounds of their different smells, echoes, taste, feel and sight. Many people experience a cross blending of the senses - sight is fused to sight, and sight to taste feel and smell. The scientific name for this trait is synesthesia. It is a cross-talk of the senses. The trait is quite common with children. If used, it can be another important catalyst to provide a vivid understanding of letter sounds.

SOUND KNOWLEDGE

Letter sound knowledge is developmental. It is built on a variety of steps to provide the child with vivid impressions to make certain that the letter sound is internalized. Various steps of the process to be followed are:

1. A reminder of what letter sounds are and what their relation is to words should be reviewed. This was previously explained, but children should be made aware of the purpose and meaning of sounds before they are formally introduced. During the child's incidental exposure to sounds, he was exposed to a variety of sounds. A reminder of sound variety can be easily provided by reminding the children of the story of *The Three Bears*. The variety of sounds from the Papa bear, the Mother bear, and the Baby bear will be a wonderful refresher.

2. Letter sound knowledge should be tied to the child's experience background as a launching point. His exposure to various readings, to games, to imaginative play will provide many letter sounds.

3. Imagineering centers can be set up in the room. These can be created around books such as Peter Pan, Winnie the Pooh, Big Pancake etc. Books are a wonderful source of the images which are the backbone of letter sounds.

4. There can be centers containing collections of various articles familiar to the children to provide letter sound games. These can be: beans, pencils, toys, sticks, books, etc. Children can bring in various objects. These can serve as objects to be used for a riddle to try out on the group.

5. Cooking sounds will help to fuse sounds to taste and to smell. Such sounds come from pumpkin, cookies, pancakes, peanut butter, etc.

6. A feeling center can be set up. This can be a table with pans of sand for tracing letters and sets of embossed letters which have had sand glued to cards. Large letters can be cut from heavy cardboard to be used for guessing the letter (after a child has been blindfolded).

7. Letter sound contracts can be duplicated and a copy given to each child.

8. Scrapbooks of letter sounds can be made of pictures cut from magazines or catalogs to illustrate specific sounds.

THE LETTER CENTER

P p

A PAINTER

...s is a painte...
...tures
...oils.
...art school.
...to paint.

Peter · Peter

Peter-Peter
    Pumpkin Eater
Had a wife and
    couldn't keep her
Put her in a
    pumpkin shell
And there he
    kept her
        very well.

3 Little Pigs

Pooh

Peter Pan

Contracts

1 2 3 4 5

LETTER SOUNDS

A a — apple	**B** b — ball	**C** c — cat	**D** d — duck	**E** e — elephant
F f — fish	**G** g — garden	**H** h — house	**I** i — Indian	**J** j — jam
K k — kite	**L** l — lamp	**M** m — mittens	**N** n — nest	**O** o — octopus
P p — pig	**Qu** qu — queen	**R** r — rug	**S** s — sun	**T** t — turtle
U u — umbrella	**V** v — vase	**W** w — wagon	**X** x — six	**Y** y — yarn
Z z — zoo	**sh** — ship	**th** — thimble	**ch** — chain	**wh** — wheel

GRAPHING

Graphing is an activity in many of the letter sound contracts. It is a valuable learning tool since it helps children develop many concepts. A few of these include:

- 1 to 1 correspondence
- seeing likenesses and differences
- classifying different attributes
- providing counting experiences
- developing "greater than," "less than" concepts
- familiarizing children with graphs

Graphing also will help develop reading skills.

- Graphing activities are designed to reinforce beginning sound knowledge. Children will be graphing and sorting objects whose sounds they are studying.
- The graphing experience will lend itself to a group experience chart. Children will therefore have additional exposure to sounds and words.

Materials:

- **Sorting Objects:** Gather objects called for on the sound contract. Pictures may be stored in manila envelopes or folders; objects may be stored in coffee cans or shoeboxes. These may be covered with colored contact paper, wall paper or construction paper if desired. No more than 10 objects of each attribute should be gathered at the start.

- **Sorting Loops:** These may be made by cutting lengths of yarn or string about 20″. Each is knotted on the end. They may also be stored in coffee cans, shoeboxes, manila envelopes or folders.

- **Graphs:** Graphs may be made so that children can physically graph each object before using a worksheet. A large graph made out of vinyl or plastic can be handy. Mark off squares and lines with a permanent marker or plastic tape. If only two attributes instead of 4 are to be used, fold the graph in half.

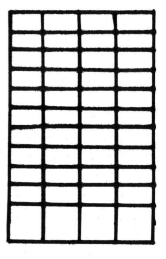

- **Worksheets:** Make copies of the appropriate worksheets needed for each child.

PROCEDURE :

1   Children look carefully at the objects.

2   They sort the objects into groups **they** think are alike. Each group has a sorting loop around it.

An additional step could be to have children count the number of objects in each loop, write it on a small piece of paper, and put it in each loop.

3   Children begin to graph each object on the vinyl graph. It may be helpful if you taped one of each of the objects to the bottom squares. Later children will be able to draw a picture of each object they will graph (or write the words!) on a separate piece of paper and place it in the appropriate bottom spaces. As children have had lots of concrete graphing experiences, they can skip using the vinyl graph and use the graph worksheet instead. This step will take time!

4   Children are now ready to plot their discoveries on the appropriate discovery worksheet. They may color or write the appropriate answers.

Experience Charts

5   After all the children in the room have graphed the objects, a group experience chart story may be written about the children's discoveries. Copies of the stories may be kept in a special "Graph Book Discoveries" booklet.

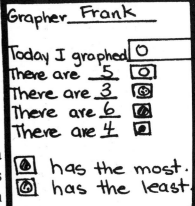

Grapher Frank

Today I graphed ⟨O⟩
There are _5_ ⟨O⟩
There are _3_ ⟨◎⟩
There are _6_ ⟨◍⟩
There are _4_ ⟨●⟩

⟨◍⟩ has the most.
⟨◎⟩ has the least.

Graphing
This week we graphed beads.
There are 5 white beads. O.
There are 3 spotted beads ◎.
There are 6 striped beads ◍.
There are 4 solid beads ●.
There are more striped beads.
The spotted beads are the fewest.
We know 6 > 3.

WORKSHEETS:

Grapher:	
10	
9	
8	
7	
6	
5	
4	
3	
2	
1	

Grapher:			
10			
9			
8			
7			
6			
5			
4			
3			
2			
1			

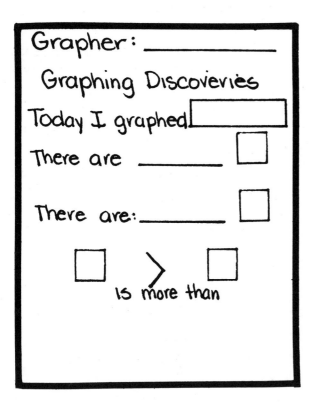

Grapher: _____

Graphing Discoveries

Today I graphed [ ]

There are _____ [ ]

There are: _____ [ ]

[ ] > [ ]
Is more than

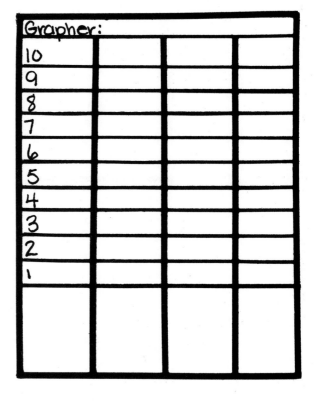

Grapher: _____

Graphing Discoveries

Today I graphed: [ ]

There are _____ [ ]

There are _____ [ ]

There are _____ [ ]

There are _____ [ ]

_____ has the most
_____ has the least

[ ] > [ ]

INTERVIEWS

Interviews can be a learning tool for developing many reading skills. A few of these skills include:

- formation of "questions"
- writing chart stories
- letter sound experiences
- developing sight vocabulary

To prepare for Classroom Interviews, begin a Human Resource File. This will become a valuable tool for you as you develop lesson plans. Information may be stored on index cards. On each card you may wish to list:

Name: Bill Jones   J.D.A.
Address: 521 Cambrian Drive
Occupation: Dentist
Pertinent Interests: African
Availability: Wednesday morn.
Telephone Number: 391-8271
Would be willing to have
the class visit his office.
Also has African slides.

In the top right-hand corner list the sound possibilities of the interviewee (last name, interest, occupation, skill, etc.). You may wish to cross file these sounds on another list. Be sure to pass out cards to teachers, friends and parents (at back-to-school night).

Questions

As the day of the interview approaches, children should develop a list of questions they would like to ask the guest speaker. These may be written on the board to be read and reread. Children may be assigned to ask each question.

We want to know:
1. Do you like your job?
2. What tools do you need?
3. How long do you have to go to school?
4. Where did you go to school?

We will interview Dr. Jones on Wednesday at 10:00.

Be sure to remember to send a group thank you note, too!

Chart Story

Following the interview, children will write a group chart story about the interview. Things that they learned from the interview may be included. The questions can be the basis for the chart story. When the story is completed, it may be added to a special Class Interview Book. You may wish to include the questions on the reverse side. The interview story may also be typed on a ditto master and put in the weekly newspaper for all to enjoy.

Class Interviews by Room 5

17

FIELD TRIPS

Field trips will provide the motivational background for a great deal of discussion. By tying them into a sound concept or unit of study they become an invaluable tool for reading and writing experiences.

Questions

Children may preceed the excursion by dictating a list of questions they wish to discover. These may be read and reread prior to the trip.

As a follow-up to the excursion, children may write a composite chart story about their expreience. Later, children develop their own individual stories. The story may be put into the class newspaper. Be sure to have children write group or individual thank yous to the helpers and people involved.

The teacher may use the experience as a basis for further chart stories. By using the same vocabulary as well as vocabulary from beginning readers, children will have exposure to the words in another context.

RIDDLE GAMES

It has been well established that there is no meaning unless the child has an image picture of the word. Images have to be from things (objects) that are a part of the child's daily life activities. This is a **must**, especially in the beginning phase of learning letter sounds, or they will be foreign for the child. Objects which are a part of the child's background of experience can be related to his play activities, from the poetry read at home and at school, from the fantasy of Mother Goose and from fairy tales, or from the many objects that have been a part of his life at home and at school (food, utensils, books, pencils, crayons, etc.). All of these have meaning for the child and so the images are stored in the library of his mind. Riddle games will be the means to provide the association of the image with the letter sound asked for in the riddle.

Sample riddles are:
1. Related to games

    "The sound that I am thinking of begins with the same sound of the thing you like to put on bread (jam), it also begins with the same letter sound of a game you play with a rope (jump)."
2. Related to school

    "The sound I am thinking of begins with the same sound as Peter's name. It is something that you use when you draw pictures on (paper)."
3. Related to home

    "It begins with same sound that you hear at the beginning of cat. It is something that mother used to put your milk in (cup)."
4. Related to fairy tales

    "I am thinking of something you use to play with--you ride in (wagon) it and it begins with the same letter sound as the animal who tried to blow the house down. (wolf)."
5. Related to Mother Goose

    "I am thinking of an animal. It begins with the same sound of an animal friend that chases mice (cat). The animal jumped over the moon (cow)."

Mother Goose Sounds

The fantasies of Mother Goose can be used to provide a visual image theatre for children. Hang various pictures of the various Mother Goose characters about the classroom. The children will love to draw and paint some of them. The pictures will provide many association cues which will echo letter sounds for children. Memory is stimulated if the association cue is ridiculous in nature. We tend to remember the unusual and to forget the common and the mundane. Mother Goose is full of the ridiculous and this is what grabs hold of the children's imagination. What could be more ridiculous than a cow jumping over the moon? Also, the main art of memory is the art of attention. The two and three dimension pictures which are played back to the child immediately holds his attention and provides a cue when a riddle is offered.

Sample questions are:

....1. "How many times do you hear the sound that robin begins with in the poem Three Blind Mice? Hold up the number of fingers you think is the answer." Read the poem to them (ran, run).

....2. Have the children point to a picture of one thing that Little Bo Peep lost which rhymes with her name (sheep).

....3. Have each child bring an object from home which is related to any thing in any Mother Goose Rhyme. They are to provide the beginning letter sound of the thing (mitten, toy, kitten, spoon, dish, etc.).

....4. Each child is to make up a riddle about Little Miss Muffett. "I am thinking of a word that tells what the spider did. It has the same sound ending that you hear in fat." (sat) Parents can be a big help here. Letters, sent home from time to time will cue them in as to what sounds are to be taught during the week.

....5. Have the children act out any Mother Goose rhyme to see if the class can guess the letter sound. Hands over eyes, look under desks, head turned up, down, side ways, etc., (look, begins same as lamp and ends same as book from Little Bo Peep).

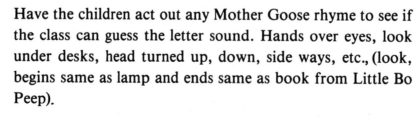

20

ALPHABET COOKING

Cooking can be not only a rewarding and enjoyable experience for children but also a richly, valuable learning tool. The possibilities for teaching sounds are endless! Since recipes can be written in chart form, it becomes an exciting approach to reading. Below are a few examples of cooking activities the class can try as they learn each new letter sound.

Aa	applesauce, alfalfa sprouts
Bb	biscuits, butter, bean salad, fried bananas
Cc	cornbread, carrot salad, cookies
Dd	dough (to make cookies), donuts
Ee	egg salad on English muffins, eggplant
Ff	french toast, french fries, fruit salad
Gg	green goddess dressing, garlic bread
Hh	honey butter on honey bread
Ii	Indian fry bread
Jj	Johnnycake, jello, gingerbread
Kk	tea from kettle, kite-shaped sandwiches
Ll	lemonade, lettuce salad
Mm	macaroni, marshmallow salad, meatloaf
Nn	noodles, nut salad
Oo	olive and cream cheese sandwich
Pp	pancakes, potato salad, pineapple, pudding
Qq	quick-a-bobs (pineapple, cheese, ham on toothpick)
Rr	raisin salad
Ss	sundaes, soup, sandwiches
Tt	tortillas, tuna, tapioca
Uu	umbrella sandwich (cut bread ↷ shape)
Vv	vegetable soup, vanilla ice cream
Ww	won tons, waffles, waldorf salad
Xx	pack box lunch for a picnic
Yy	yoghurt
Zz	zucchini muffins, fried zucchini

Aa

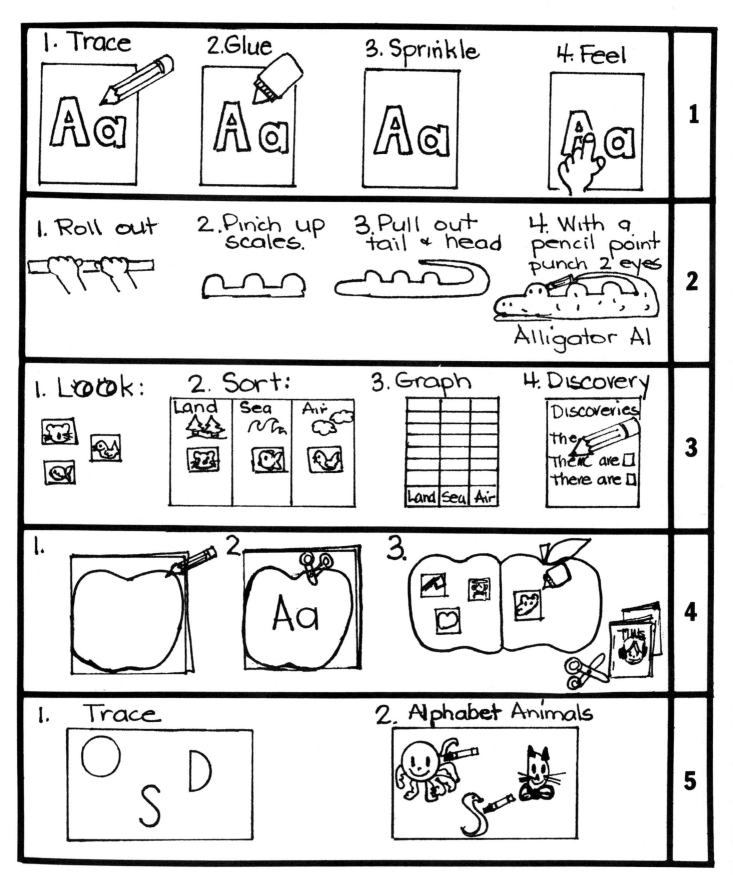

Row 1: 1. Trace | 2. Glue | 3. Sprinkle | 4. Feel

Row 2: 1. Roll out | 2. Pinch up scales. | 3. Pull out tail & head | 4. With a pencil point punch 2 eyes — Alligator Al

Row 3: 1. Look: | 2. Sort: (Land, Sea, Air) | 3. Graph (Land, Sea, Air) | 4. Discovery — Discoveries the There are ☐ there are ☐

Row 4: 1. | 2. Aa | 3.

Row 5: 1. Trace (O S D) | 2. Alphabet Animals

CONTRACT MATERIALS and
PROCEDURES:

1 9″ × 12″ light-colored construction paper, pencils, "Aa" tagboard letter patterns, Adhesive sticker dots (available at stationery and variety stores)

2 Alligator Al

Provide a ball of green claydough or clay for each child. Children follow the sequence as shown on the contract to make Alligator Al. Claydough may be made by mixing: 1 cup flour, ½ cup salt; gradually add ⅓ cup water (which has green food coloring added to it). Bake on a foiled cookie sheet in a slow oven until done.

3 Sort Animal Pictures

Provide a group of animal pictures. Children sort them on the sorting chart as to where they live: land, sea, air. Pictures may then be placed in rows on a large paper graph or checked off on a graph worksheet. Discoveries are then filled out on a Graph Discovery worksheet for each child.

4 Apple Books

On a folded 12″ × 18″ paper, children trace a tagboard apple pattern. Keeping the paper folded, children cut out the apple keeping the fold intact. A green construction paper leaf may be added to the front of the apple. Pictures of "Aa" sounds cut from magazines are glued inside the Apple Book.

5 Alphabet Animals

On a 12″ × 18″ piece of construction paper children trace their choice of tagboard letter patterns. With crayons, children decorate the letters into animals.

More A Activities

SOUND OBJECTS:

anchor   ax   apple   ant

SPECIAL INTERVIEW:

acrobat,   actress,   actor,   attorney

SPECIAL FIELD TRIP:

In the afternoon visit an animal (athlete, acting school, admiral, printing shop to see alphabet).

TALKING TIME:

If you could be any animal, what would you be? Why?

DISCOVERY: Observe an anthill

MOVEMENT: Be an acrobat!
Animal Walks: crab, duck, elephant, snake

ANIMALS: Alligator, Ants

PROJECT: Children sit in a circle. Pass around a box of animal cookies. Children randomly take one. They must tell a ''story'' about the animal and then they may eat it.

VOCABULARY: anchor   antenna   alphabet   admiral   absent

Bb

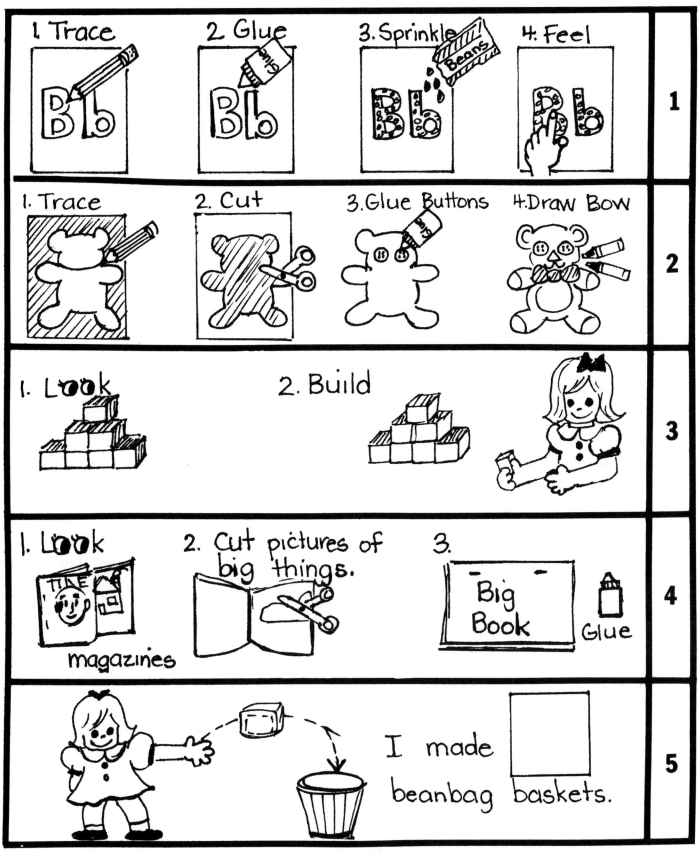

CONTRACT MATERIALS and PROCEDURES:

1 9″ × 12″ light-colored construction paper for each child, glue and pencils; "Bb" tagboard letter patterns, bag of beans.

2 Make Brown Baby Bear with Button eyes and a Bow from 9″ × 12″ brown construction paper for each child.
Make a bear pattern for children to trace around out of heavy paper such as tagboard.
Glue, pencils, scissors, crayons, buttons for eyes.
Details such as the bow, nose and mouth are drawn.

3 Block Buildings
Build 5 block structures for children to duplicate out of matching blocks. Block cubes, wood scraps or children's blocks may be used. Each child is to try and construct your exact constructions.

4 Big Book of Big Things
Make a large blank scrapbook from 12″ × 18″ construction paper. Fill it with blank drawing paper including enough sheets for each child. Staple the book pages. Title the book "Big Book" with a marking pen. Provide magazines and catalogs for children to cut. Children paste pictures of things they find that are big on their own page. Teachers may help children "spell" the picture words under each picture!

5 Beanbag Baskets
Provide beanbags and a wastepaper basket at the station. A masking tape line may be put down to toss behind. Children see how many baskets they can make. The number is written in the square.

More B Activities

SPECIAL INTERVIEW: boys in the room. (bus driver)

Each day select a few boys to interview.

Children may wish to ask the boys:
- Where were you born?
- What do you like to do?
- What is your family like?

SPECIAL FIELD TRIP: the bakery.

SCIENCE DISCOVERIES: bubbles.

Make a mixture of detergent and water.

Provide each child with a straw. Discoveries:
- What makes the bubbles move?
- What makes the colors?
- Where else do you see these colors?

MOVEMENT: balloons.
- Blow up balloons and knot them. How long can you keep the balloon in the air?
- Play balloon toss.
- Ball bouncing activities.

TALKING TIME: When are you bossy?

SPECIAL WORDS:

beautiful (What is beautiful to you?)

boil (What makes water boil?)

SPECIAL CLASS PROJECT: Helium Balloons

Each child writes a message on a small piece of paper. Such as: "Please write me if you find this" followed by the child's name and address. Write each message on a plastic bag. Attach each message to a helium balloon with a string tied to the message and the balloon. Let all the balloons go at once for a beautiful sight!

Cc

1
1. Trace
2. Glue
3. Sprinkle Cornmeal
4. Feel

2
1. Look: Look around
2. Cut "C" Pictures
3. Make a Collage of C things.

3
1. Trace
2. Cut
3. Glue yarn
4. Draw cat

4
1. Look caps
2. Sort
3. Graph
4. Graph Discoveries Discoveries I graphed There are ☐ There are ☐ There are ☐

5
1. Look: Catalogue
2. Cut 5 pictures of things you like ☺
3. 1. 2. 3. 4. 5. them to show which you want the most and the least.

CONTRACT MATERIALS and PROCEDURES:

1 9″ × 12″ light-colored construction paper for each child, glue and pencils, box of cornmeal. "Cc" tagboard letter patterns.

2 "C" Collage
Provide magazines, coloring books, workbooks, scissors and glue. Children cut pictures of things beginning with a "c" sound. Each child arranges his/her own patterns on a cardboard sheet in a collage. Cotton and corduroy as well as other "c" textures may also be used.

3 9″ × 12″ yellow construction paper for each child. Two tagboard circle patterns for children to trace for cat head and body - one circle slightly larger than the other. Each child cuts 2 small triangle ears, body, head and tail from the yellow. These are glued to form cat shape. Whiskers may be added from cut paper strips, yarn or pipecleaners. Features are drawn in with crayon.

4 Cap Graphing
Save an assortment of four different kinds of bottle caps. Children will sort and graph these.
—Graph, sorting loops, pencils.
—Graph discovery ditto for each child.

5 Ordering Favorites
Each child cuts out 5 favorite things from a catalogue. Following your sample he/she writes the numbers from 1 to 5 on a 9″ × 12″ sheet of paper. Each child must decide which of the five selections he/she likes the most and least. These are glued accordingly on the paper.

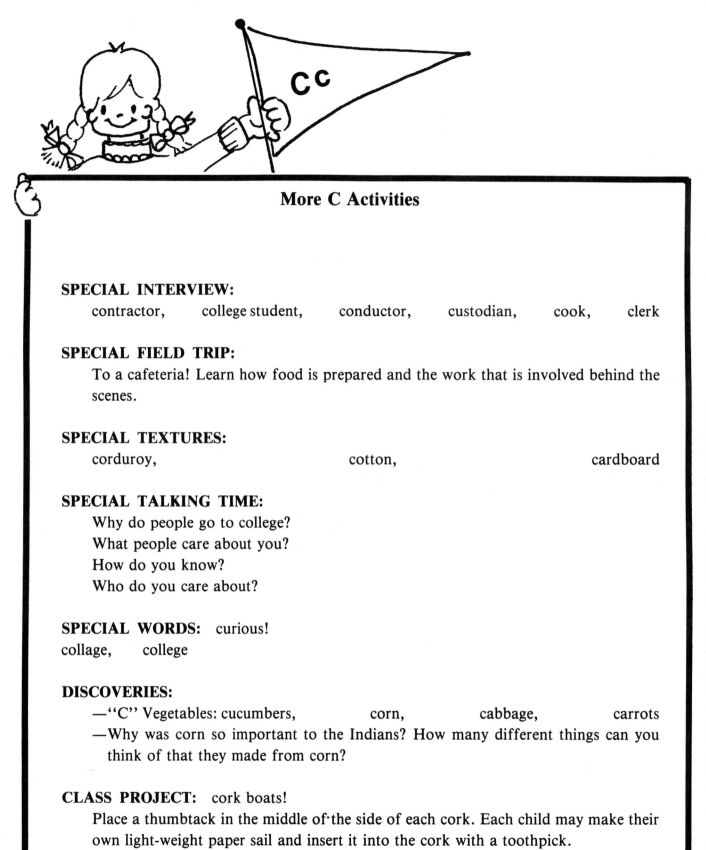

More C Activities

SPECIAL INTERVIEW:

contractor,   college student,   conductor,   custodian,   cook,   clerk

SPECIAL FIELD TRIP:

To a cafeteria! Learn how food is prepared and the work that is involved behind the scenes.

SPECIAL TEXTURES:

corduroy,   cotton,   cardboard

SPECIAL TALKING TIME:

Why do people go to college?
What people care about you?
How do you know?
Who do you care about?

SPECIAL WORDS: curious!

collage,   college

DISCOVERIES:

—"C" Vegetables: cucumbers,   corn,   cabbage,   carrots
—Why was corn so important to the Indians? How many different things can you think of that they made from corn?

CLASS PROJECT: cork boats!

Place a thumbtack in the middle of the side of each cork. Each child may make their own light-weight paper sail and insert it into the cork with a toothpick.
What makes them move in a tub of water?

Dd

Row 1:
1. Trace
2. Glue
3. Sprinkle — sawdust
4. Feel

Row 2:
1. Paint a scene inside.
2. Make clay dinosaurs.
3. Put leaves in clay.

Row 3:
1. Trace
3. Glue

Row 4:
1. Look:
2. Sort:
3. Graph
4. Discoveries

Discoveries
There are
The
There are ☐
There are ☐

Row 5:
1.
2. 'Dd staple cut.
3. or Dd Pictures

CONTRACT MATERIALS and PROCEDURES:

1 9″ × 12″ construction paper/child, glue, pencil, "Dd" letter patterns, sawdust.

2 Dinosaur Diorama

Each child decorates his own diorama in a shoebox. Background is painted with blue and green paint. Clouds may be added by gluing cotton to the box. Green Easter basket grass may be added to the bottom. Dinosaurs are made out of clay. Small leaves may be stuck into clay for "bushes".

3 Daisies

Children trace a large circular pattern on yellow construction paper. Petals are traced onto orange paper. The patterns are cut and glued into a daisy. Features are added with construction paper.

4 Sorting Dinosaurs

Provide plastic dinosaurs available in variety stores for children to sort. Children group the dinosaurs in the sorting loops. Children may make up their own variables: kind of dinosaur, color, habitat, and plot on the graph worksheet. Children may then fill out their discoveries on the Discovery Worksheet.

5 Diamond Dd Book

Children trace a diamond tagboard pattern on two pieces of 9″ × 12″ colored construction paper. The covers are stapled together along the sides. Children cut out Dd pictures from magazines or draw them and paste them inside the book.

More D Activities

SOUND OBJECTS

daisy, drum, doll, dog
diamond, daffodil, duck, dinosaur

SPECIAL INTERVIEW:

doctor, dentist, dad

SPECIAL FIELD TRIP:

downtown, dairy, duck farm

TALKING TIME:

Why is your Dad special to you?
Describe your dad.

SCIENCE DISCOVERY: dinosaurs

SPECIAL ANIMALS: duck, dog, dinosaur, deer, donkey

VOCABULARY: dozen, danger, decide, defeat

READING TIME:

Danderlion by Don Freeman, Viking Press, New York, 1964.

WRITING TIME: Suppose you went back in a time capsule to dinosaur days. What would you see?

E e

Row 1: 1. Trace · 2. Glue · 3. Sprinkle — egg-shells · 4. Feel

Row 2: staple · Draw Ee pictures

Row 3: 1. Trace · 2. Decorate · 3. Embroider the Egg

Row 4: 1. Look · 2. Sort · 3. Graph · 4. Discoveries — eggs — Graph Discover / There are / There / There are □ / There are □

Row 5: 1. Color · 2. Cut · 3. Staple · 4. Stuff — Crumble paper

CONTRACT MATERIALS and PROCEDURES:

1 9″ × 12″ light-colored construction paper/child, pencils, glue, broken egg shells, "Ee" tagboard letters.

2 Elephant Books
Children trace around an elephant tagboard pattern on two pieces of 9″ × 12″ **red** construction paper. The pattern is also traced around 5 pieces of newsprint. The pages are cut out and stapled between the red front and back covers. Each child draws pictures of Ee things.

3 Egg Embroidery
Precut burlap into 9″ × 12″ pieces for each child. Masking tape may be overlapped around the edges to prevent fraying. They may also be stitched around the edges to prevent fraying. With a marking pen, children trace around a tagboard egg pattern on the burlap. Simple designs are also drawn. Each child then embroiders the designs with light-weight colored yarn. Large plastic needles are available at variety stores for children's use.

4 Egg Sorting
Provide an assortment of plastic colored Easter eggs (available at variety stores) to sort and graph. Children sort by color.
Graph. Sorting loops, discovery worksheet for each child.

5 Eskimo Doll
Make a ditto of an Eskimo Doll such as the picture on the contract. Run this off on 9″ × 12″ white construction paper. Children cut the pattern and a blank piece of white paper. Decorate the doll with crayons. Children staple the doll half-way around and stuff the "inside" with crumbled newspaper pieces. Staple closed.

More E Activities

SPECIAL INTERVIEW: engineer, employee, employer, Eskimo, exercise leader, someone with an Ee name
(Ellen, Eddie, Emily, Esther, Ethel, Elmer ...).

SPECIAL FIELD TRIP: Eskimo exhibit, art exhibit, chicken ranch to see eggs

SPECIAL CLASS PROJECT:
hatch eggs in an incubator

TALKING TIME:
"What do you enjoy doing?"
"What things are an effort to you?"

VOCABULARY: effort, employ, embroider

MOVEMENT: exercise!

ART PROJECTS: egg carton animals

SPECIAL STUDIES: Eskimos
Invite someone to show their slides of Eskimos.

DRAMATICS: Entertain the class with a play: The Little Red Hen.

ANIMAL: elephant

FUN PROJECT: Dye eggs like the Russians.

OBJECTS: elf, embroidery, egg, Eskimo, elephant, envelope

F f

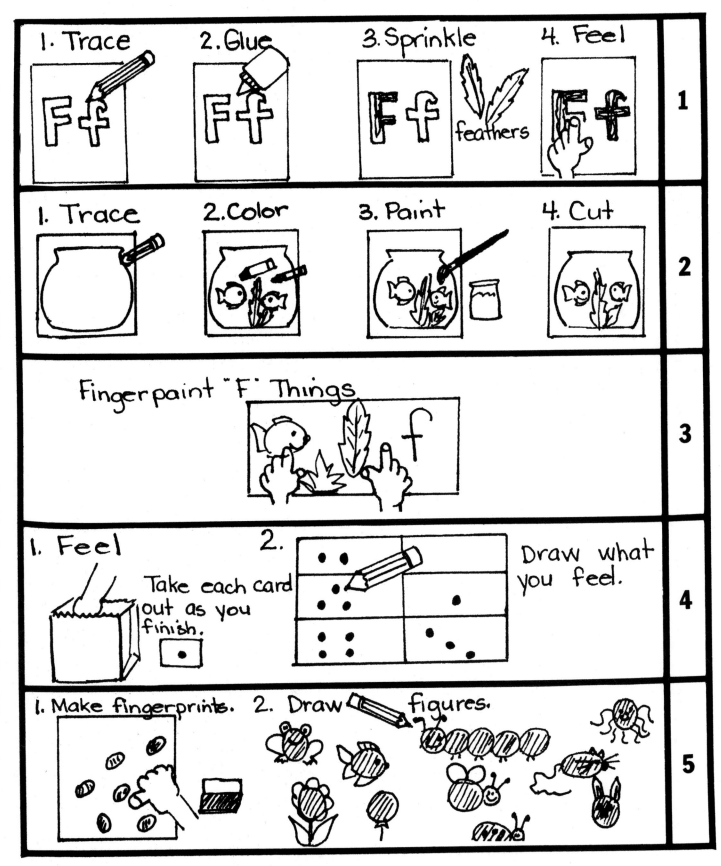

1

1. Trace   2. Glue   3. Sprinkle   4. Feel   feathers

2

1. Trace   2. Color   3. Paint   4. Cut

3

Fingerpaint "F" Things

4

1. Feel   Take each card out as you finish.   2.   Draw what you feel.

5

1. Make fingerprints.   2. Draw figures.

CONTRACT MATERIALS and PROCEDURES:

1 9″ × 12″ light-colored construction paper for each child, pencils, glue, feathers, "Ff" patterns.

2 Fish
9″ × 12″ white construction paper for each child; fish bowl tagboard pattern to trace around. Each child traces shape then draws heavily with crayon a "fish-bowl" scene. Prepare a "white-wash" paint with a few teaspoons of blue tempera paint mixed in a jar with a quart of water. Children lightly "paint" over their fish bowl. When dry, the fishbowl may be cut out and pasted on a 9″ × 12″ piece of colored construction paper.

3 Fingerpainting "F" Pictures.
Each child spreads a few tablespoons of liquid starch on a piece of 9″ × 18″ construction paper. Spread a few tablespoons of thick liquid paint on the paper. Children fingerpaint "f" pictures.

4 Feely Bags
Make five feely cards by using 4″ × 6″ index cards. Place blobs of white glue in circular shapes on the cards in 1-6 number patterns. When the glue dries the blobs will harden. Place these inside a paper bag. Children carefully feel each card without looking. When they have determined what the number configuration is, children draw what they felt on a teacher-made ditto as above. They may check themselves by looking at the card.

5 Fingerpaints! On a 9″ × 12″ piece of white construction paper, each child makes fingerprints using an ink pad. Thin felt pens are used by the child to make "creatures ".

More F Activities

SPECIAL INTERVIEW:
father, fireman, farmer, forest ranger

SPECIAL FIELD TRIP:
farm, fire department

SPECIAL TALKING CIRCLE:
What is a friend to you?
What is special about your father?

VOCABULARY:
forestry, fabulous, famous, fossils, float, fins

SPECIAL SCIENCE DISCOVERIES:
What animals have feathers?
Did you know that no one else in the world has the same fingerprints as you? Examine fingerprints.

ANIMAL DISCOVERIES:
fox and fish
Why do fish have fins?

SPECIAL STUDY: fossils
What are fossils?

"Fossils" can be made by pouring plaster of Paris into small tins. While still soft chicken bones, shells, marbles and sticks may be added to give a "fossil" look.
Pull these out just before hardening.
Pull off the aluminum and each child will have their very own "fossil".

Gg

1.

1. Trace   3. Sprinkle   4. Feel

green glitter

2.

1. Trace   2. Cut   3.

Tell a ghost story to a grown up. She will write it down.

3.

1. Look: girls   boys

2. Sort

3. Graph

4. Discovery Paper

Graph Disc
I gra
there are ☐
There are ☐

4.

1. Cut a hole in the lid 3"x 3".

2. Wrap 5 rubber bands on the box.

3. Strum the guitar to the beat of the record.

5.

1. Trace ○

2. green grass

3. green stems green leaves

4. Glue glitter to make a garden.

CONTRACT MATERIALS and PROCEDURES:

1 9″ × 12″ light-colored construction paper for each child, glue and pencils, green glitter, "Gg" tagboard letters.

2 Ghost Stories
12″ × 18″ white construction paper for each child. Tagboard pattern of a ghost, scissors, pencil. Each child makes their own "ghost" by tracing the pattern and cutting it out. Each child then dictates a story about a ghost to a grown-up who writes it down in full story form. Later children may search for "Gg's" in their story.

3 Graphing Girls (and Boys)
On small index cards write the name of each child in the class. A small picture of the child may be pasted on the back of the cards for "readability." Children sort the cards into groups of boys or girls.
—Graph, sorting loop, graphing discovery ditto/child.

4 Guitar
—Shoebox for each child, 5 rubber bands for each child. The start of a 3″ × 3″ hole in the top lid of each box is started by an adult. Each child may complete his own circle and wrap 5 rubber bands over the hole and around the box. Children may practice strumming their guitars to the beat of a record set up on a record player and a listening post.

5 Green Glitter Garden with Grass made from Glitter (a Gate may be added too with grasshoppers!)
—12″ × 18″ construction paper for each child.
Circle shapes to trace around (large spools are ideal)
—6″ × 9″ green construction paper/child for green grass, stems and leaves. When these have been pasted down, children may add glue and glitter to the inside portions of the flowers.

More G Activities

SOUND OBJECTS:
glue   green   gun   guitar   glitter   gourd   grasshopper   gate

SPECIAL INTERVIEW:
grandmother,   grandfather,   guitarist,   special girl,   gardener,   garbage man

SPECIAL FIELD TRIP: grocery store

TALKING TIME: "What is great about me?"

SCIENCE DISCOVERIES: grass
"Plant" green grass seed on a dampened sponge and watch it grow!
Plant a flower garden in milk cartons.

ANIMAL DISCOVERIES: grasshoppers and gorillas, goats

SPECIAL WORDS: gorgeous and graph

CLASS PROJECTS:
- Act out the Three Billy Goats Gruff.
- Play Guessing Games about G words:
   "I'm thinking of a "G" word that is a color. What is it?"

SPECIAL DISCOVERIES: Green
What two colors when mixed together make green? Can you discover it?

Hh

Row 1: 1. Trace — 2. Glue — 3. Sprinkle (holes, holepunch) — 4. Feel

Row 2: 1. Trace — 2. Cut — 3. Staple — 4. Color — House Books

Row 3: 1. Look: hair in room. — 2. Sort Color. (red, yellow, Black, Brown — Sue, Tad, Bill, Nan, Sue, Sally, Carol, Greg, Cindy, Nancy, Jack, Dan) — 3. Graph (red, brown, yellow, black) — 4. Graph Discoveries (Discoveries I graphed There are ☐ There are ☐)

Row 4: 1. Look Hh. (Look, TIME) — 2. Cut Hh — 3. Put in ♡.

Row 5: 1. Trace — 2. Cut 2. — 3. Punch (yarn) — 4. Lace (h)

CONTRACT MATERIALS and PROCEDURES:

1 9″ × 12″ light-colored construction paper for each child, glue and pencils, "Hh" tagboard letters, hole punch and light-weight paper to punch "holes" to glue on Hh.

2 House Book
Provide a house-shape pattern like shown on the contract for children to trace around on 2 pieces of 9″ × 12″ white construction paper. Provide pre-cut drawing paper cut the size of the rectangular shape of the house. Each child staples five sheets of this paper inside the front and back cover he/she has cut. The "outside" cover is colored just like the child's house. Each inside page the child depicts a different room inside his house.

3 Graphing Hair Color
On small index cards write the name of each child in the class. A small picture of each child may also be pasted on each card to aid the non-reading child. Cut a small piece of construction paper of each of the following colors: red, yellow, brown, black. Children sort the name cards into the sorting loops by hair color (represented by the color strips).
—Graph, sorting loops, pencils.
—Graph discovery ditto for each child.

4 Hh Pictures
Children draw or cut out Hh pictures from magazines or coloring books. The pictures are put inside the Hh. (You may wish to stipulate the number of pictures to be found.)

5 Lace-Up Heart
9″ × 12″ red or pink construction paper - 2 for each child.
Tagboard heart pattern to trace around.
Each child traces and cuts out two red hearts. With a hole punch, holes are punched half-way around (top left opened). Each child laces up the hearts with yarn. Decorate with crayons.

More H Activities

SOUND OBJECTS

playhouse	hose	handkerchief	horse	hand
hats	hanger	hippopotamus	happy	hair

SPECIAL INTERVIEW:

harpist, hospital worker, happy person

SPECIAL FIELD TRIP:

hospital, hardware store, house being built

TALKING TIME:

"I hate it when....."
"I feel happy when....."
"Things that are hard for me are....."

MOVEMENT:

hopping, hobble, hunch

SPECIAL DISCOVERIES:

human heart
how a house is built

DISCOVERY GAMES: heavy

Put five different weighted objects in paper bags (rock, cotton, handful of rice, wood, ruler)
By "feeling" weight, children order the bags from lightest to heaviest.

VOCABULARY: horrendous, heavenly

GAMES: Use hats!

Line up five hats. Children look at them carefully.
Scramble the hats. Children unscramble them to the correct original order.

I i

1
1. Trace
2. Glue
3. Sprinkle — glitter
4. Feel

2
1.
2. brown
3. block
4. red

3
1. Trace letters
2. Stitch running-stitch around initials.

4
Use: [ruler].

How many inches?

hand   desk   pencil   paper

5
1. Trace
2.
3.
4. Cut pictures
Ii things.

46

CONTRACT MATERIALS and PROCEDURES:

1 9″ × 12″ pink construction paper for each child, glue, pencils, "Ii" tagboard letter patterns, glitter to sprinkle on glue.

2 Indian Boy
9″ × 12″ brown construction paper for each child. Children trace around circular tagboard pattern on brown paper. Using black construction paper scraps, children cut hair and round eyes and glue onto face. Red headband and mouth is cut from red paper. The headband is decorated with crayons. A feather is cut from bright-colored construction paper and glued on.

3 Stitchery Initials
On a square precut burlap (8″ × 8″) piece, children trace their initials from the tagboard letter patterns using an ink pen. Adhesive tape may be overlapped around the edges to prevent fraying. Using colored yarn, children use a running stitch to outline their initials. Large needles may be purchased at a variety store.

4 Inches
Using an inch-ruler, children measure the length of their hand, the length of their desk, pencil and their contract to determine how many inches each is. The answers are written in the squares.

5 Igloos
A 12″ × 18″ piece of white construction paper is folded in two for each child. Children trace around igloo pattern keeping one edge on the fold. Children cut along the open edges, and glue pictures of "Ii" objects cut from magazines in the inside. The cover is colored as an igloo.

More I Activities

SOUND OBJECTS:
plastic Indians, .ink, igloo, insect, infant

SPECIAL INTERVIEW:
illustrator, Indian
Invite friends to share their instruments. Children in an upper grade may enjoy this.

SPECIAL FIELD TRIP: an instrument store

SPECIAL TALKING TIME:
If you could invite anyone to your house who would you ask?
Imagine you are twenty years older. What will you be doing?

SPECIAL VOCABULARY: infection, imagination, interrupt

SPECIAL ANIMAL: iguana, insects

SPECIAL STUDY: Indians

INQUIRY: instruments
Invite friends to share their instruments. Children in an upper grade may enjoy this.

SPECIAL ART PROJECT: make an igloo out of marshmalows or sugar cubes.

J j

1.
1. Cut 2. Spread Jelly 3. Eat!

2.
Listen Gingerbread Boy

3.
1. Trace 2. Cut 3. Decorate
- ◉◉ buttons
- ～～～ ric rac
- glitter
- crayons
- paper

4.
1. Look: jellybeans
2. Sort:
3.
4. Graphing Discoveries
I graph
then
There are ☐
There are ☐
There are ☐

5.
1. Look:
2. Find:

49

CONTRACT MATERIALS and
PROCEDURES:

1 Piece of bread for each child, knives, jam and jelly, cardboard letter pattern of "Jj" teacher-made.

2 Gingerbread Boy
Record or tape-book set of Gingerbread Boy:(Tape may be made by teacher.) Listening post, ear phones, tape recorder (or record player). Each child follows story along in book.

3 Make Gingerbread Boy
Brown 9″ × 12″ construction paper for each child. Gingerbread boy pattern to trace. Each child makes their own gingerbread boy. Decorations may be made from ric rac, glitter, tissue, buttons, and scrap paper. Provide glue, scissors and pencils.

4 Jellybean Graph
Provide an assortment of four different colors of jelly beans to sort and graph. Graph, sorting loops, graphing discovery ditto for each child.

5 Jars and Lids
Provide a large assortment of jars with screw-on lids. These may be stored in a large box at the center-station. Unscrew the lids from the jars. Children find the appropriate lid to each jar and screw them on.

More J Activities

SPECIAL INTERVIEW:
gymnast, janitor, juggler, jeweler

SPECIAL FIELD TRIP: Japanese gardens
to a jewelry store
jar bottling plant

SPECIAL ANIMALS: Jungle Animals.
jaguar, giraffe

SPECIAL FEATURE: Invite someone in to show their films of Japan.

SCIENCE DISCOVERY
What is a jungle?

MOVEMENT: Jumping

SPECIAL CLASS PROJECT:
How many jellybeans do you think are in the jar?

SPECIAL TALKING TIME:
"If you could go anywhere you wanted on a Magic Jet where would you go? Why?"

WORDS: gigantic, jungle

SPECIAL STUDY: Jupiter

K k

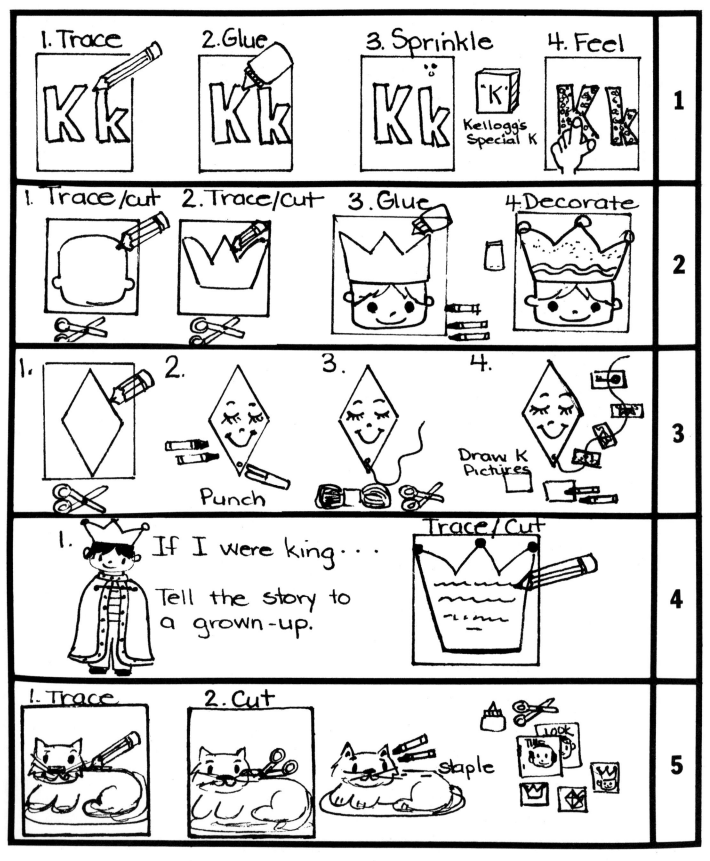

Row 1:
1. Trace
2. Glue
3. Sprinkle — "K" Kellogg's Special K
4. Feel

Row 2:
1. Trace/cut
2. Trace/cut
3. Glue
4. Decorate

Row 3:
1.
2. Punch
3.
4. Draw K Pictures

Row 4:
1. If I were king... Tell the story to a grown-up.
Trace/Cut

Row 5:
1. Trace
2. Cut
staple — look

CONTRACT MATERIALS and PROCEDURES:

1 9″ × 12″ light-colored construction paper, glue, pencils, "Kk" tagboard letter patterns, Kellogg's Special "K" cereal.

2 King
9″ × 12″ flesh colored construction paper for each child to trace face pattern on, king's crown pattern to trace on gold wrapping paper. Patterns are cut and glued accordingly. The crown is decorated with glitter, sequins, ric rac, etc.

3 Kites
Children trace around a tagboard kite pattern on bright-colored construction paper. Features are added with crayon and a small hole is punched in the bottom of the kite. A yarn tail is tied to the hole. Children draw or paste Kk sound pictures on small squares of papers. These are pasted to the tail.

4 "If I Were King..."
Children trace a crown pattern on 12″ × 18″ yellow construction paper. The crown may be decorated with glitter, sequins and ric rac, and then cut out. Each child dictates a story to a grown up telling what they would do if they were king and could make any changes they wanted.

5 Kitten Book
Children trace around a tagboard kitten pattern on two pieces of yellow construction paper. The kitten is cut out and outlined with crayon. The cover is stapled together on the top. Children draw or paste Kk sound pictures inside the Kitten Book.

More K Activities

SOUND OBJECTS:
    kangaroo, keys, kite, king, kitten

SPECIAL INTERVIEW: Invite someone to show their slides of Australia and see kangaroos and koala bears.

SPECIAL FIELD TRIP: to the pet store to see new kittens

SPECIAL PROJECT: fly a real kite!
    Children can then write stories about the kites. Pretend you are the kite.
    What did you see when you were in the air?

TALKING TIME:
    If you were king and could make any rules or changes you wanted what would you do?
    What would the perfect kingdom be to you?

SPECIAL ANIMALS: kangaroo, kittens, koala

SORT: keys!

L l

Row 1:
1. Trace
2. Glue
3. Break leaves
4. Feel

Row 2:
1. Look — Lincoln Logs
2. Build

Row 3:
1. Look: leaves
2. Sort:
3. Graph
4. Discoveries — I Discovered / There are ☐ / there are ☐ / There are ☐

Row 4:
1. eyes / nose / ears
2. glue / cotton / lamb

Row 5:
1. Vein side up
2. Rub leaves with crayons.

CONTRACT MATERIALS and
PROCEDURES:

1 9″ × 12″ lilac colored construction paper, glue, pencils, "Ll" tagboard letter patterns, leaves to break-apart and glue on.

2 Lincoln Logs

Build five Lincoln Log constructions. Each child reproduces the log cabin buildings exactly using additional Lincoln Logs.

3 Leaf Graphing

Provide an assortment of four different kinds of leaves to sort.
—Sorting loops, graph, pencils.
—Graphing discovery ditto for each child to fill out.

4 Lambs
—Paper plate for each child.
—Large supply of cotton balls.
—Glue, scissors, paste.
—Construction paper scraps: blue, white.
Children cut eyes, nose and ears out of construction paper and paste them onto the plate. A mouth is added from red yarn or colored paper. Cotton balls are pasted on the plate in such a manner so that the plate is not seen and features are not covered.

5 Leaf Rubbings

Children may collect leaves on nature excursions and from home. These are kept at the station. Leaves are turned veinside up. 12″ × 18″ white construction paper is placed over the leaves. Using "leaf colors" gently color back and forth over the leaves until the imprint shows.

More L Activities

SPECIAL OBJECTS:

leaves	lamb	lion
lemon	lanterns	licorice
logs	lollipops	letters

SPECIAL INTERVIEW: librarian, lawyer

SPECIAL FIELD TRIP: library

SPECIAL TALKING TIME: Who do you love?

ANIMALS: lion, lamb, lizard, ladybug

CLASS PROJECT: "Listening Walk"
Come back to draw all the things heard on the walk.

SCIENCE STUDY:
What makes light?
Why do leaves fall?
How do leaves drink?
What makes leaves green?

VOCABULARY: lovely, lucious, livid, listen, lanterns:
How did they work?
When were they used? Why?

SORTING: little things, long things

MOVEMENT: Make your body be...
low, little, long

SPECIAL DISCUSSION:
What helps us listen?

M m

1. Trace   2. Glue   3. Sprinkle   4. Feel

1

Sort the Mail

Mm   Mm

2

1. Trace   2. Cut   3. Punch   4. Cut

L   R   L   R   Tie

3

1. Look: 2. Build:

Marshmallow Structures

4

M Mobiles

1.   2.   3. Punch   5.

Cut   Draw M pictures   4. Cut

5

CONTRACT MATERIALS and PROCEDURES:

1 9" × 12" light-colored construction paper for each child, glue and pencils; "Mm" tagboard letter patterns; bag of small macaroni.

2 Sort the Mail!

Draw or paste pictures of things beginning with the sound "m" on envelopes. Make several pictures that do not begin with this sound. Fold a 12" × 18" piece of construction paper in half. On one side write "Mm" and on the other side write "Mm." Children sort the mail appropriately. If available, a mailman's hat is fun to wear. You may wish to make more than one game for several children to use.

3 Making Mittens!

Children trace their left and right hands with thumb extended and four fingers together on 9" × 12" light-colored construction paper. Mittens are cut out and L (left) and R (right) are drawn on the appropriate mitten. Small holes are punched in the lower part of each mitten and they are tied together with yarn.

4 Marshmallow Structures

Build 5 marshmallow structures for children to duplicate out of marshmallows (large kind) and toothpicks. Each child is to try and construct your exact buildings using marshmallows and toothpicks.

5 "M" Mobiles

Make a ditto of 5 different shapes on a piece of construction paper. Children cut out the shapes draw a picture of something that begins with M on each shape. A small hole is punched in each shape. 5 lengths of string are cut to tie the shapes onto the hanger.

More M Activities

SOUND OBJECTS:

money	marbles	mask
milk (carton)	magnet	marshmallow
mouse	mirror	magnifying glass

SPECIAL INTERVIEW:

mailman, milkman, minister or mother

SPECIAL FIELD TRIP:

Take a trip to a post office to see how mail is sorted and delivered.

SPECIAL DISCOVERIES:

1. magnets — Why do they work and what things do they pick up. Children may sort items into two groups at a center.
2. magnifying glass — Children may look at marbles or money using a magnifying glass. How does it change things?
3. microscope — What is it?

SPECIAL WORDS:

magnificent! and marvelous
What makes things melt?

SPECIAL TALKING TIME:

1. What makes you mad?
2. What is special about your mother?

SPECIALS:

Remember to march to music!
Look in a mirror to see how special you are.
Measure yourself!

Nn

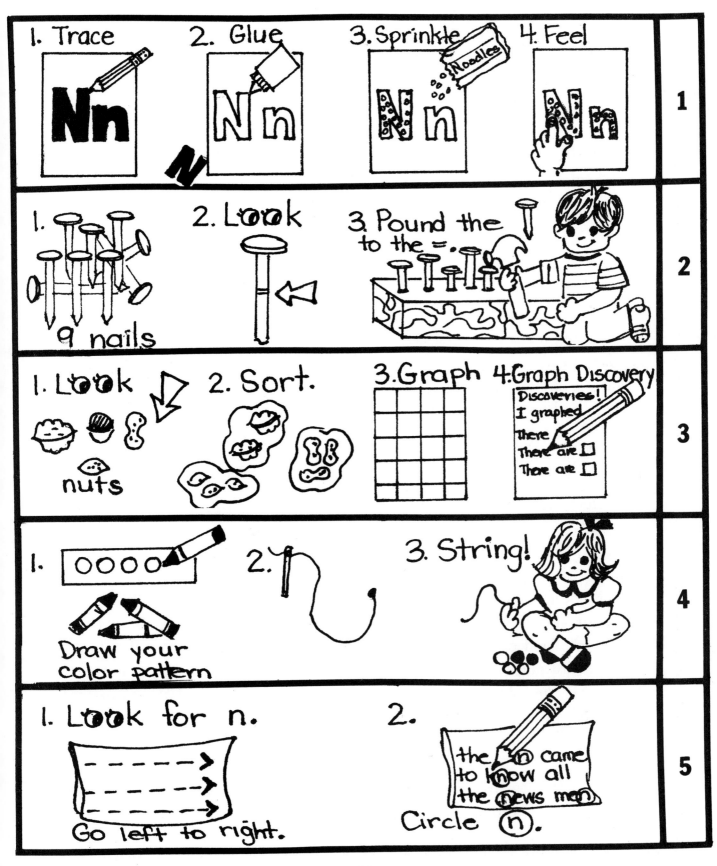

1.
1. Trace
2. Glue
3. Sprinkle — Noodles
4. Feel

2.
1. 9 nails
2. Look
3. Pound the ⊤ to the =.

3.
1. Look
2. Sort. nuts
3. Graph
4. Graph Discovery — Discoveries! I graphed ___ There ___ There are ☐ There are ☐

4.
1. Draw your color pattern
2.
3. String!

5.
1. Look for n. Go left to right.
2. the n came to know all the news men. Circle n.

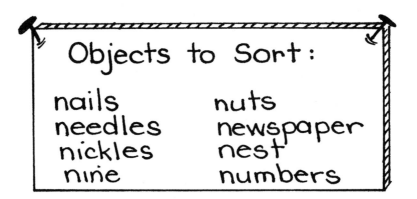

CONTRACT MATERIALS and PROCEDURES:

1 —9″ × 12″ light-colored construction paper for each child,
—glue and pencils
—bag of small noodles
—"Nn" tagboard letter patterns

2 —A large supply of nails.
—Mark a line on each nail with a red marking pen
Vary the location on each nail.
—Provide a few thick boards and hammers.
Each child counts nine nails. Keeping his/her eye on the red mark, the child tries to hammer in each nail only to the line.

3 —A selection of different kinds of nuts to sort: acorns, almonds, peanuts, walnuts
—Graph, sorting loops, pencils
—Graph discovery ditto for each child.

4 Nifty Noodle Necklaces strung with a Needle!
—In four glass jars mix five tablespoons of vinegar and a few drops of one color of food coloring per jar: red, blue, green and yellow. Put a large handful of macaroni (the kind with the holes in it) in each jar, screw on the lid tightly and shake! Pour the colored macaroni on sheets of wax paper to dry. Precut heavy thread and knot each end. Large needles are available in variety stores. Each child may first draw the necklace pattern on a paper strip.

5 Cut a 4″ × 6″ piece of newspaper for each child. Each child begins at the top left of the paper and slowly moves his eyes from left to right. Each N is circled.

More N Activities

SOUND OBJECTS:

nails	nickels	nuts	numbers
needles	nine	nests	newspaper

SPECIAL INTERVIEW: The Nurse

Invite the school nurse to the classroom. Children may discuss ahead of time what kinds of questions they may want to ask.

•What do you do?

•Do you like your work?

•What do you have to do to learn how to be a nurse?

A group chart story may be written about these findings.

SPECIAL FIELD TRIP: Newspaper Office

Visit a newspaper office to see how a newspaper is printed. A chart story may be written about the trip.

SPECIAL THING TO DISCUSS: Nice

What things are nice to you?

SPECIAL TEXTURE TO DISCUSS: Nylon

•How does it feel?

•What season would you wear it in?

•Do you have anything made out of it?

SPECIAL DISCOVERY: Bird nests!

Show picture books of nests and, if possible, display real bird nests.

Oo

1. Trace 2. Glue 3. Sprinkle 4. Feel Cherrios	1
My experience with an octopus! ...	2
Trace Staple Cut Look "O" sounds	3
1. 2.	4
1. ⬤ the pattern. 2. String an O Necklace Straw cherrios straw	5

64

CONTRACT MATERIALS and PROCEDURES:

1 9″ × 12″ light-colored construction paper, glue, pencils, "Oo" tagboard letter patterns, box of Cheerios.

2 Octopus Encounter
Each child cuts the top of a 9″ × 12″ piece of light blue construction paper like waves. He/she dictates to a grown-up about a pretend under-water encounter with an octopus. The story is written on the waves.

3 Olive Book
Children trace an olive shaped pattern on two pieces of light-green construction paper. The shapes are then cut out and stapled on the edge. Children draw or paste Oo sound pictures inside the book!

4 Underwater Scene
On a 12″ × 18″ piece of white construction paper, each child depicts an underwater scene using crayons. Remind children to color heavily and fill in as much of the white as possible. Children lightly paint over the underwater scene using a paint solution of 1 tablespoon of blue poster paint and 1 pint of water.

5 "O" Necklaces
Each child draws a necklace pattern on a rectangular card using "O" and ⌷ ." Children may then string the pattern on a length of yarn using a large needle. Small strips of paper straws and Cheerios may serve as the "beads."

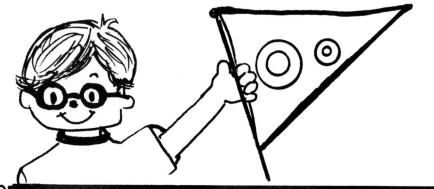

More O Activities

SOUND OBJECTS:
olive, oxen, octopus, ostrich

SPECIAL INTERVIEW: optometrist, ophthalmologist (eye doctors), author

SPECIAL FIELD TRIP: visit an office, opera

TALKING TIME: opposite
What does opposite mean?
What words would you use to tell someone about you?
Think of things that are opposite what you are.

SPECIAL ANIMALS: octopus, oxen, ostrich, ocelot, otter

SPECIAL DISCUSSION: What is special about you? What do you deserve an Oscar for?

VOCABULARY: opposite, optical, occupy, optimist, obstinate, octane

SCIENCE: Discuss how we breathe.
Why do we need oxygen?
What part of our body helps us breathe?
What do fish use to breathe?
What do we use if we swim underwater?

P p

1. 1.Trace 2.Glue 3. Bend — pipecleaners 4.Feel

2. Potato Prints with Pink Paint — dip in pink paint

3. 1. Look: paper clips 2. Sort: 3. Graph 4. Discoveries — Discoveries I gra... Th... There are ☐ There are ☐

4. 1.Trace 2. Cut 3. Glue — pink yarn

5. 1. Trace 2. Cut 3. Staple 4. Draw "P" Pictures

CONTRACT MATERIALS and PROCEDURES:

1 9″ × 12″ pink construction paper for each child, pink pipecleaners, glue and pencils, "Pp" tagboard letters.

2 Potato Prints with Pink Paint
"Premake" potato print designs with a sharp knife an half a potato. 12″ × 18″ purple construction paper for each child. Pie-tin filled with pink paint. Children may dip potatoes into paint, wipe-off excess, and press down on paper...continue to form a picture.

3 Paper Clip Graphing
A selection of different sized paper clips.
—Graph, sorting loops, pencils.
—Graph discovery ditto for each child.

4 Pink Popcorn Pig
Pre-pop popcorn with red-food coloring in the pan with the kernels. Make a tagboard pig pattern. Children trace the pattern on 9″ × 12″ pink construction paper. Cut out the pig and paste pink popcorn on the pig. A small pink tail may be made out of yarn.

5 Purple Purse
Fold a 12″ × 18″ piece of purple construction paper in half. Each child traces a tagboard purse pattern on the fold. Cut the purse out along the top and sides (not the fold). Staple along the sides. Add a pink yarn handle stapled in place. Each child draws five pictures of Pp things on cut squares of pink paper and put them in the purse.

More P Activities

SPECIAL INTERVIEWS:
   pilot, publisher, poet, printer, paint

SPECIAL FIELD TRIP:
   to the park, paint store, pizza place, planetarium, printing press

TALKING TIME:
   "What is pretty to you?"
   "What present would you most like?"

CLASS PROJECTS:
   a puppet show!

FAVORITE BOOK: Peter Pan

SPECIAL ANIMALS: pig, penguin, pigeon

ART PROJECT: Pebble People
   Paint small features with acrylic paint on river pebbles.

SCIENCE PROJECT: pumpkins
   Cut apart a pumpkin with the class.
   Save the seeds to dry and then roast on a cookie sheet. (Sprinkle with salt)
   Have a guessing game of how many seeds there are. Cut open a pineapple and eat!

SPECIAL FUN: Pop popcorn and put inside a box decorated as a present. Wrap it so the
   lid comes off. Pass the present around the circle saying, "Open the present, What do
   you see? Open the present, but don't tell me!" Each child takes a peek. When all have
   had a peek, eat the popcorn!

Qu qu

Row 1: 1. Trace 2. Glue 3. Sprinkle 4. Feel

Row 2: 1. Trace/Cut 2. Trace/Cut 3. Glue 4. Decorate

Row 3: 1. Glue Hair 2. Decorate 3. Glue 4. Quilt

Row 4: 1. 2. Qu qu / queen / quilt / quail

Row 5: 1. Look 2. Sort: 3. Graph 4. Discoveries — Discoveries there are ☐ / there are ☐ / there are ☐ / there are ☐

CONTRACT MATERIALS and PROCEDURES:

1 9″ × 12″ light colored construction paper, pencil, glue, "Qq" tagboard letter patterns, box of Quaker Oats.

2 Queen

Tagboard face pattern to trace on 9″ × 12″ flesh colored construction paper. Queen's crown pattern to trace on foil or gold wrapping paper. Patterns are cut out and pasted accordingly. The crown is decorated with glitter, sequins, ric rac, etc. The queen's face may be decorated with crayon.

3 ME Quilt

Each child decorates a pre-cut pink or flesh colored 6″ circle to look like them. Yarn representing their hair color is glued on. Button eyes, hair ribbons, lace collars, felt noses and red yarn mouths are added to the faces. The completed faces are glued to denim 8″ × 8″ squares. A volunteer stitches each square together for the completed ME Quilt.

4 Quills

In a class demonstration, cut the tip of a feather with a razor in such a manner as to make a pen-tip. Children may then practice using the quill to make Qq's by dipping the quill into ink.

5 Sorting the Queen of Hearts

Take several decks of cards and use only the heart suit. Make up sorting packs by using the Queen of Hearts, Jack, King and Ace. Children sort these into groups in the sorting loops, graph them and then write their discoveries.

More Qu Activities

SOUND OBJECTS:
quilt, quill, Quaker Oats, quarter

SPECIAL INTERVIEW: Invite someone in to show you how they made a quilt.

SPECIAL FIELD TRIP: Quietly go to the library.

TALKING TIME:
Talk about a time something made you quiver.
Tell how you feel when you quarrel.

SPECIAL ANIMAL: quail.

VOCABULARY: quiver, quarter, quality

DISCUSSION: When do you use a question mark? Think of questions to ask a friend.

DISCUSSION: Why do we use money?
How is money made?
Who is the person on a quarter?
Why was he important?

R r

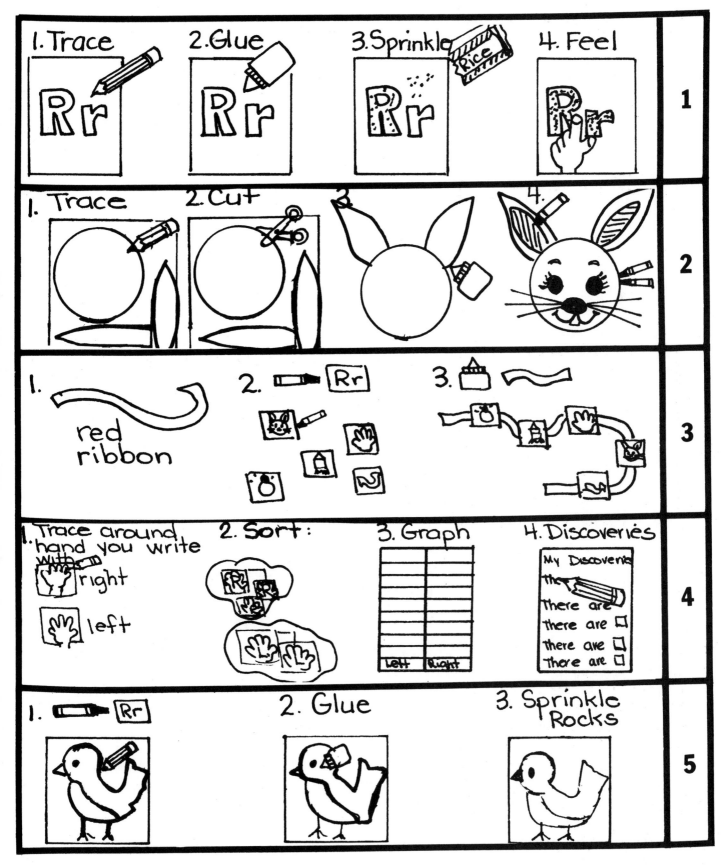

Row 1: 1. Trace 2. Glue 3. Sprinkle *Rice* 4. Feel

Row 2: 1. Trace 2. Cut 3. 4.

Row 3: 1. red ribbon 2. Rr 3.

Row 4: 1. Trace around hand you write with: right / left 2. Sort: 3. Graph (Left Right) 4. Discoveries — My Discoveries / There are □ / there are □ / there are □

Row 5: 1. Rr 2. Glue 3. Sprinkle Rocks

CONTRACT MATERIALS and

PROCEDURES:

1 9″ × 12″ red construction paper for each child, glue, pencils, "Rr" tagboard letter patterns, bag of rice to sprinkle.

2 Rabbit

Children trace circle face and ear patterns on a 12″ × 18″ piece of white construction paper. The tracings are cut out and glued as shown in figure 3. Features including eyes, nose and mouth may be added by using colored construction paper or crayons. Whiskers may be made from pipecleaners, yarn or construction paper strips.

3 Red Ribbon

A strip of red ribbon is pre-cut for each child. On pre-cut red construction paper squares each child draws five or more pictures of "Rr" sounds. These pictures are pasted on each child's ribbon.

4 Sorting Right and Left Hands

Each child traces around the hand he/she writes with on pre-cut paper squares. Each child sorts the hands into right or left hand groups in the sorting loops. The pictures may then be placed on a large graph or children may check off each picture on a worksheet graph. Discoveries are then filled out on the Graph Discovery Worksheet.

5 Rock Pictures

Each child draws an Rr sound picture on a cardboard square. The picture is then filled in with glue. Children sprinkle colored rocks on their pictures to complete the "rock portrait".

More R Activities

SOUND OBJECTS:

rug	rock	rice	ruler	red
ribbon	ring	rabbit	rose	rug

SPECIAL INTERVIEW: real estate salesman
writer

SPECIAL FIELD TRIP: Walk down the road to look for "Rr" sounds and make rubbings.

TALKING TIME:
What resolution would you make?

SPECIAL ANIMALS: rabbit, reindeer, rat, robin

SPECIAL STUDIES: rockets, rain, roots

VOCABULARY: reflection
"I look in the mirror
and what do I see?
A very special person
because it is me!"

MATH: rectangles
How many things can you see shaped like a rectangle?
Cut out rectangles and make pictures out of them.

Ss

Row 1:
1. Trace
2. Glue
3. Sprinkle sand
4. Feel

Row 2:
1. Trace
2. Look — Human Body
3. straws
4. Glue Skeleton

Row 3:
1. Look: Suckers
2. Sort:
3. Graph
4. Discoveries — Graph Discov. / There are ☐ / There are ☐ / There are ☐ / There are ☐

Row 4:
1. 'S' Picture
2. Stitchery — yarn

Row 5:
1. S Picture
2. Glue
3. Stick Seeds

CONTRACT MATERIALS and PROCEDURES:

1 9″ × 12″ light-colored constuction paper, glue, pencils, sand, "Ss" letter patterns.

2 Straw Skeleton
On a 9″ × 12″ flesh-colored construction paper children trace a tagboard "paperdoll." Provide human body models, books/filmstrips for children to look at the skeleton. Children cut white paper straws into smaller sections. These are glued on the body outline to represent "bones" and the skeletal frame.

3 Sort Suckers
Provide an assortment of different colored suckers to sort and graph. Sorting loops, graph, graph discovery worksheet for each child.

4 "S" Stitchery
Provide each child with a square burlap piece. Masking tape may be overlapped around the edges to prevent fraying. Each child draws something depicting "S" with an ink pen (felt) on the burlap (a silly sun, sailboat in the sea, starfish in the sand). Using a large needle and colored yarn, children use a "running stitch" to outline their picture. Large needles are available at variety stores.

5 Seed Pictures
On cardboard squares children draw a picture of an object beginning with an "S". The inside of the picture is covered with glue. Children fill the picture with different kinds of seeds.

More S Activities

SOUND OBJECTS:

soap	seeds	stone	Santa	spoon
suckers	straw	sock	spider	

SPECIAL INTERVIEW: school secretary
stewardess, sailor

SPECIAL FIELD TRIP: to the store (how many "S" things can you find?)

SPECIAL TEXTURE: silk

TALKING TIME:
What makes you feel silly?
What do you want from Santa?
What makes you smile?
What makes you sad?

VOCABULARY: submarine, silver, signal

SPECIAL ANIMAL: squirrel, snake, seal, spider

SCIENCE: What makes snow?
Make snowflakes.
How do you hear sound?

SPECIAL STUDY: the seal

sand,	sand dollar,	sailfish,	salmon,
starfish,	sailboat,	sailor,	submarine,
sun,	snail,	sink,	sailfish

T t

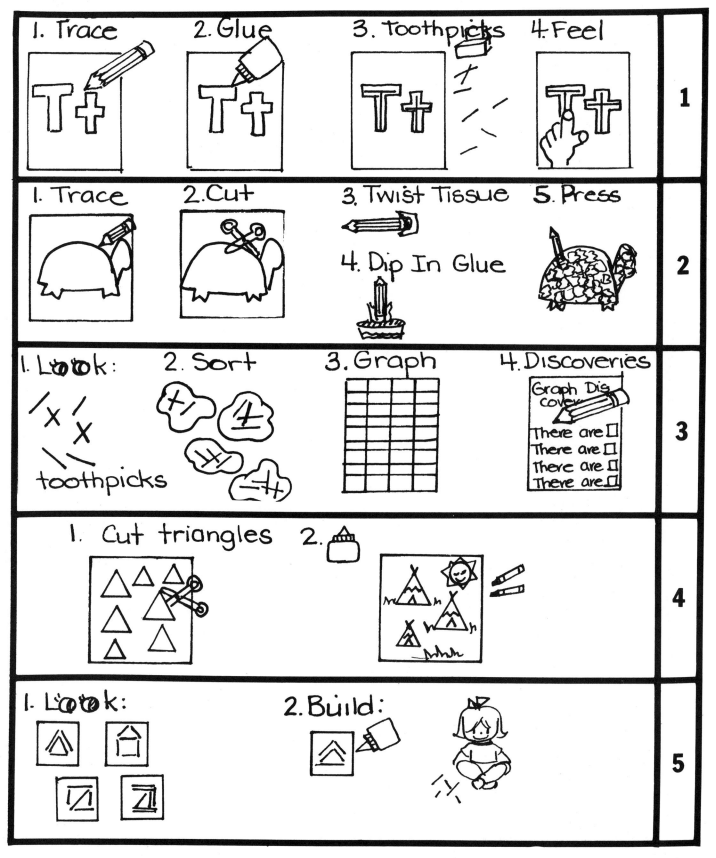

Row 1:
1. Trace   2. Glue   3. Toothpicks   4. Feel

Row 2:
1. Trace   2. Cut   3. Twist Tissue   4. Dip In Glue   5. Press

Row 3:
1. Look: toothpicks   2. Sort   3. Graph   4. Discoveries

Graph Discovey
There are ☐
There are ☐
There are ☐
There are ☐

Row 4:
1. Cut triangles   2.

Row 5:
1. Look: 2. Build:

CONTRACT MATERIALS and
PROCEDURES:

1 9″ × 12″ light-colored construction paper, glue, pencils, ''Tt'' tagboard letter patterns, toothpicks.

2 Tissue Turtle
Children trace a tagboard turtle pattern on 9″ × 12″ construction paper. Cut the turtle out. Children wrap small pre-cut tissue paper squares one by one, around a pencil eraser. The tip of the tissue is dipped into glue and then pressed onto the turtle. Continue until all of the turtle is covered.

3 Graphing Toothpicks
Provide a supply of colored toothpicks. Children may sort and graph the toothpicks on the basis of color.
—Sorting loops, graphs, discovery graph worksheet for each child.

4 Triangle Pictures
Provide a ditto of differing-sized triangles run-off on a piece of light-colored construction paper. Triangle patterns may be provided instead for children to trace. Children cut them out and paste them on a 12″ × 18″ piece of light-colored construction paper. Using crayons, children decorate their pictures forming a picture using the shapes.

5 Toothpick Designs
Make a few simple toothpick designs by gluing them on squares of black construction paper. Children duplicate the designs by gluing toothpicks on pre-cut black construction paper squares.

More T Activities

SOUND OBJECTS:

turtle	toothpick	ten	tiger
top	tack	tape	truck

SPECIAL INTERVIEW: teacher

SPECIAL FIELD TRIP: T.V. station

SPECIAL ANIMALS: turtle, tiger, turkey, toad

SPECIAL TALKING TIME:

What things do you like to talk about?
What is terrifying to you?

SCIENCE DISCOVERY:

What helps us talk?
Why do we have a tongue?
How do we taste?
How many teeth do we have?

VOCABULARY: triangle, terrific, terrifying

MOVEMENT: be tiny and tall
Exercise doing "touch toes."

DISCOVERY: temperature
Each day look at a thermometer to see what the temperature is?

DISCUSSION:

Is it important to take turns?
Tell about a time you felt terrible.

MATH: Telling time

U u

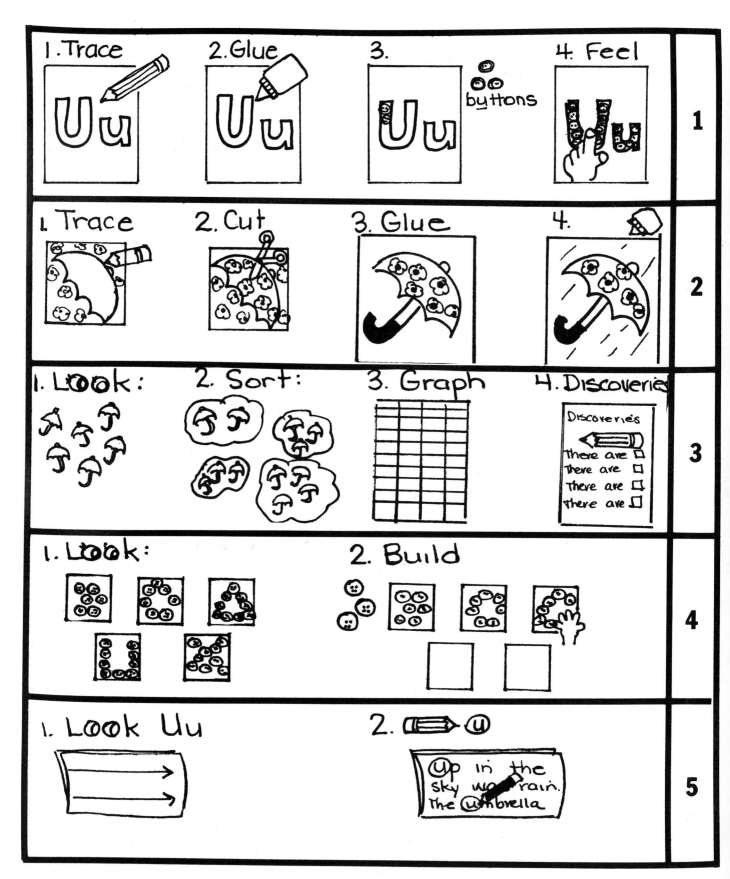

Row 1:
1. Trace
2. Glue
3. buttons
4. Feel

Row 2:
1. Trace
2. Cut
3. Glue
4.

Row 3:
1. Look:
2. Sort:
3. Graph
4. Discoveries

Discoveries
there are ☐
there are ☐
there are ☐
there are ☐

Row 4:
1. Look:
2. Build

Row 5:
1. Look Uu
2. ✏️ → Ⓤ

Up in the sky was rain. The umbrella

CONTRACT MATERIALS and
PROCEDURES:

1 9″ × 12″ light-colored construction paper for each child, glue, pencils, "Uu" tagboard letter patterns, buttons.

2 Umbrellas
Children trace an umbrella pattern on wallpaper. The umbrella is cut out and glued on a 9″ × 12″ piece of blue construction paper. Glue is glued in streaks on the blue paper to act as "rain".

3 Sorting Umbrellas
Provide several packages of colored umbrellas available at variety stores. Children take turns sorting these by color, and grouping them in the sorting loops. Findings are then marked on graph worksheets (or set on a large graph). Each child then fills out an individual discovery worksheet.

4 Button Designs
Make at least 5 designs using buttons. Glue these designs on 6″ × 6″ squares of black construction paper. Children duplicate the designs on plain black construction paper squares. If enough buttons are not available, children do not need to glue them on.

5 Tracking "Uu"
Cut a 4″ × 7″ column of newspaper for each child. Children are to look carefully on each row from left to right then return to the next row, etc. Searching for "Uu." Each time a Uu is found it is circled with a pencil. Children may enjoy trying a new paper they have not seen and track with a sandtimer. They can see how many "Uu's" they found before the sand ran out.

83

More U Activities

SOUND OBJECTS:
umbrella, umpire, buttons

SPECIAL INTERVIEW: Invite someone's Uncle to come and talk to the class.
Also...an umpire!

SPECIAL FIELD TRIP: Go to a movie where an usher helps you.
Go someplace unknown, go upstairs, or under an under pass .

TALKING TIME:
What things upset you?
Tell about a time when you were upset.

VOCABULARY: umpire. What is an Uncle?
unequal

LEARN TO: to tie and untie your own shoes.

LISTEN TO: *Umbrella* by Tara Yashima.
Viking Press, New York.
Write a group story about a rainy day.
The Ugly Duckling, by Hans Christian Anderson.

V v

85

CONTRACT MATERIALS and PROCEDURES:

1 9" × 12" violet construction paper for each child, glue, pencils, velvet pieces to cut up, "Vv" letter tagboard patterns.

2 Violet Vase

Children trace around a tagboard pattern of a vase and cut it out. The vase is decorated with paint (lace, ric rac, glitter and crayon designs may be added). Flowers may be cut from wallpaper floral designs or made from construction paper. These are glued above the vase onto green paper strips.

3 Vests

Children cut straight up the middle of the front of large paper bags. A neck opening is cut in an oval shape in the top of the bag. Two arm hole openings are cut in the sides of the bag. Children may then decorate their bag vest with crayons and then wear it.

4 A "V" Vine

Children paste green yarn on a 12" × 18" piece of violet construction paper to look like a "vine." Children cut 5-7 green leaves from green construction paper. On each leaf, draw pictures of "V" things. The leaves are glued on the vine.

5 Valentine Creatures

Children trace a tagboard "valentine" pattern on a 12" × 18" violet piece of construction paper. Children make valentine-shaped animals, plants or "things" out of crayons.

More V Activities

SOUND OBJECTS:
vaseline   vessel   van   valentine
velvet   vase   vest

SPECIAL INTERVIEW: veterinarian, volunteer worker at the school, vision expert (ophthalmologist, optometrist), violinist, veteran

SPECIAL FIELD TRIP: Vet hospital (animal),
visit the village; visit a vegetable market.

SPECIAL TEXTURE: velvet

TALKING TIME:
1. What is valuable to you?
2. If you could visit anywhere where would you go?
3. Where is your favorite vacation place?

SCIENCE DISCOVERY: Venus

CLASS PROJECT: Vegetable soup!
Each child brings a vegetable to school.
Cut them up and add chicken broth and herbs.
Cook into a vegetable soup!

SPECIAL ANIMAL: vulture

ART PROJECT: Make a milk carton village.

VOCABULARY: vote, vanish, village, vessel, value, variety, various, volume

W w

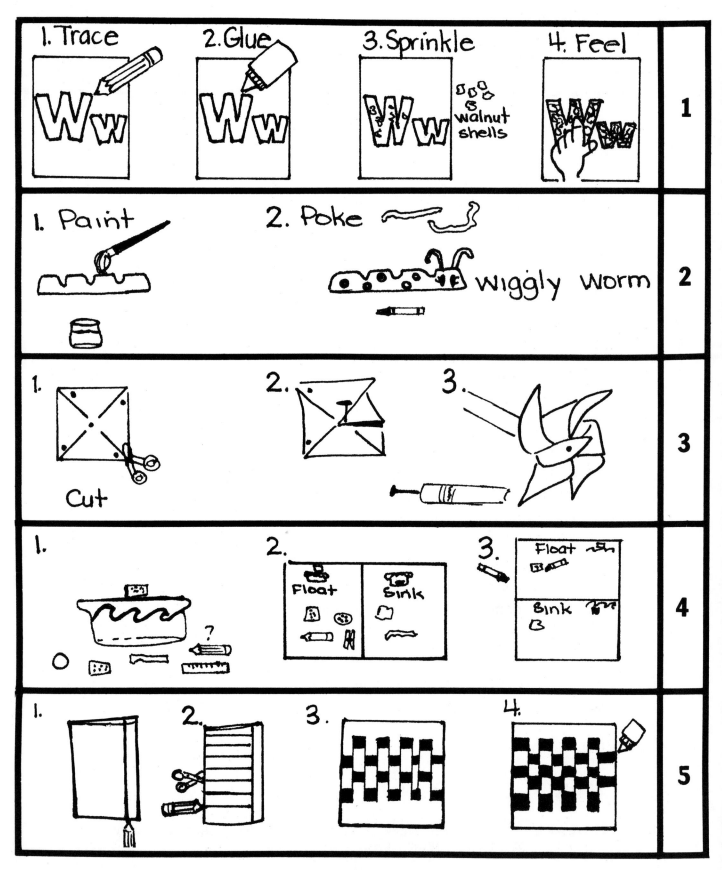

Row 1:
1. Trace
2. Glue
3. Sprinkle — walnut shells
4. Feel

Row 2:
1. Paint
2. Poke — wiggly worm

Row 3:
1. Cut
2.
3.

Row 4:
1.
2. Float / Sink
3. Float / Sink

Row 5:
1.
2.
3.
4.

CONTRACT MATERIALS and PROCEDURES:

1 9″ × 12″ light-colored construction paper, glue, pencils, "Ww" tagboard letter patterns, walnut shells.

2 Wiggly Worm
Each child paints a 4 section strip of an egg carton that has been cut down the center.
Two pipecleaners are stuck in the top of the "worm." Spots and eyes are added with crayon.

3 Pinwheels
Make a ditto of a pinwheel (figure 1) for each child. Run it off on colored paper. Children cut along the lines nearly to the center without creasing the paper, children gently "fold" up each piece to the center placing a pin in the middle. Push the pin into the eraser end of a pencil. (figure 3).

What makes it turn? Blow on it.

4 Float and Sink (in Wet Water)
Provide a small tub half-filled with water. In this, children can experiment with various objects to discover whether they sink or float. Objects can include: a cork, pencil, rock, chalk, magnet, paper clip, ruler, ball, stick, clothespin, sponge, etc., 12″ × 18″ construction paper (figure2) with "float" and "sink" written on to sort accordingly and (figure 3) a worksheet for children to draw which objects floated and sank.

5 Paper Weaving
Fold a colored paper 12″ × 12″ in half (figure 1) and draw a line 1″ from the edge. Using a ruler draw lines perpendicular to the edge line 1″ apart (figure 2). Children cut on the lines. Using paper strips pre-cut (12″ × 1″) children weave in and out of the spaces. Glue down "flaps ".

89

More W Activities

SOUND OBJECTS:

wagon, window, windmill, water,
worm, witch, wax paper, web

SPECIAL INTERVIEW: a special woman

SPECIAL FIELD TRIP: Take a nature walk.

Collect objects in a bag for each child. Each child can make their own collage by "ironing" the objects between two pieces of wax paper.

TALKING TIME:

If you could have any wish, what would you wish for?

SPECIAL ANIMALS: walrus, wolf
Watch a web.

SPECIAL DISCOVERY: silk worms

SCIENCE: Wind
1. Children can make walnut boats from half a walnut shell. In the bottom put a small amount of clay. Cut a triangular paper sail. Put a toothpick in it and stick it in the clay.
2. Put the boats in the water tub.
   Does it move?
   How can you make it move?
   What happens if you blow too hard?
3. Discuss the effects of wind on sailboats and glidders.
4. What is a tornado?

X x

Row 1:
1. Trace
2. Glue
3. Sprinkle
4. Feel

Row 2:
1. Cut six pictures.
2. Put between wax paper.
3. Iron (Teacher help)

Row 3:
1. Trace
2. Make a silly animal.
3. Color

Row 4:
1. Punch 2 holes in each shoebox.
2. Cut 2 strings 36" each. Tie knots
3. Walk

Row 5:
1.
2. Staple Cut.
3. Tell a story about a fox with an axe.

CONTRACT MATERIALS and PROCEDURES:

1 9″ × 12″ construction paper for each child, pencils, glue, "Xx" tagboard letters, Trix cereal.

2 Wax Collage
Children find 6 pictures or nature objects that they like. They arrange the objects between two pieces of 9″ × 12″ wax paper. The teacher presses the collage together with a warm iron.

3 X Animal
Children trace around a large tagboard X on a 9″ × 12″ paper. Each child makes a silly animal on the shape and colors it with crayons.

4 Shoebox Fun
Have each child bring in 2 shoeboxes from home. Prepunch 2 holes in the middle of the long side of each box. Children measure off 36″ on a yardstick, using heavy string. The two pieces of 36″ string is cut and tied in each hole. The child puts his feet in the boxes while holding the string in his hands, and then walks carefully.

5 Axe Book
Each child traces around a tagboard axe pattern on 2 pieces of 9″ × 12″ construction paper. The pattern is also traced around several pieces of plain writing paper. The pages are stapled between the construction paper cover. The child dictates a story about a fox with an axe to the teacher. The story is written inside the book.

More X Activities

SOUND OBJECTS:
box, fox, six, axe, Lux, Trix, toybox, Jack-in-the-box

SPECIAL INTERVIEW:
X-Ray technician

SPECIAL FIELD TRIP:
X-Ray laboratory

SCIENCE DISCOVERY:
How wax is made.
Mixing different paints to discover how colors are formed.

SPECIAL ANIMALS:
ox, fox

VOCABULARY:
xylophone, X-ray

READING TIME:
Henny Penny, The Gingerbread Boy, The Big Pancake all have a fox character. The teacher reads the stories to the class and then discusses with the class the fox character. Various types of words to describe the fox are listed. He has the same characteristics in each story (sly, wise, cunning, etc.).

PLAY TIME:
Put on a class play about The Fox and the Grapes (Aesop Fables).

Y y

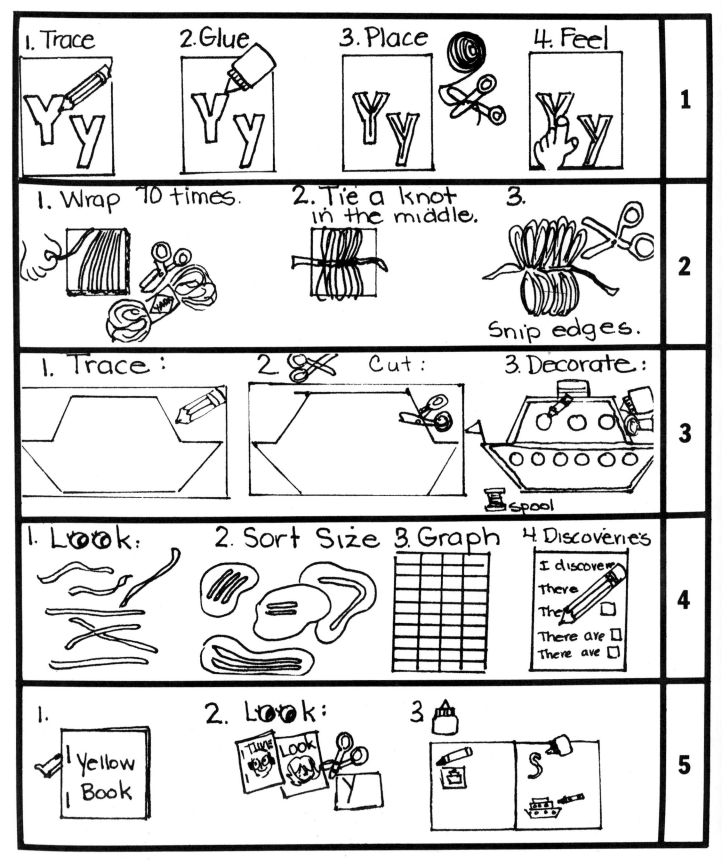

1
1. Trace 2. Glue 3. Place 4. Feel

2
1. Wrap 10 times. 2. Tie a knot in the middle. 3. Snip edges.

3
1. Trace : 2. Cut : 3. Decorate : spool

4
1. Look: 2. Sort Size 3. Graph 4. Discoveries
I discover
There
The
There are
There are

5
1. Yellow Book 2. Look: 3.

CONTRACT MATERIALS and PROCEDURES:

1 9″ × 12″ yellow construction paper for each child, glue, pencils, yellow yarn, "Yy" tagboard letter patterns.

2 Yellow Yarn Balls

Each child wraps yellow yarn around pre-cut 5″ × 5″ cardboard squares 70-100 times. Children gently tie a knot in the middle of the yarn on each side of the cardboard. They gently slide the yarn off the cardboard on their fingers. Snip along the edges until each is opened. Fluff up!

3 Yellow Yachts

Children trace a yacht pattern on a 12″ × 18″ yellow construction paper and cut it out. The yacht is decorated by gluing bright-colored yarn along the edges. Port holes may be made by tracing around a spool or dipping the spool into paint and making "spool prints." A flag may be added.

4 Sorting Yarn

Cut four colors of rug yarn into four definite lengths. Children sort the yarn on the basis of length. Discoveries are graphed on the graph worksheet and on the Discovery Worksheet.

5 Yellow Book

Each child makes their own Yellow Book by folding 12″ × 18″ construction paper (yellow!) in half. The titled "Yellow Book" is printed on the front. Pictures of Yy sounds cut from magazines are pasted inside. Children may also draw their own pictures.

More Y Activities

SOUND OBJECTS:
yarn, yacht, yellow, yo-yo

SPECIAL INTERVIEW:
yoga expert, "your" friend

SPECIAL FIELD TRIP: yoghurt store,
your home

TALKING TIME:
What do you remember about this year?
What do you remember about being young?

CLASS PROJECT: Make a yearbook
Each child can make his own page showing what they remember most about the year. They can each draw pictures about themselves. Children can take turns thinking of reasons why they like their friends. Run these off on a ditto and add a yellow cover strung together with yellow yarn.

ANIMALS: yak, yellow bird

SCIENCE DISCOVERY: Hatch eggs in an incubator. What happens to the yolk?

Z z

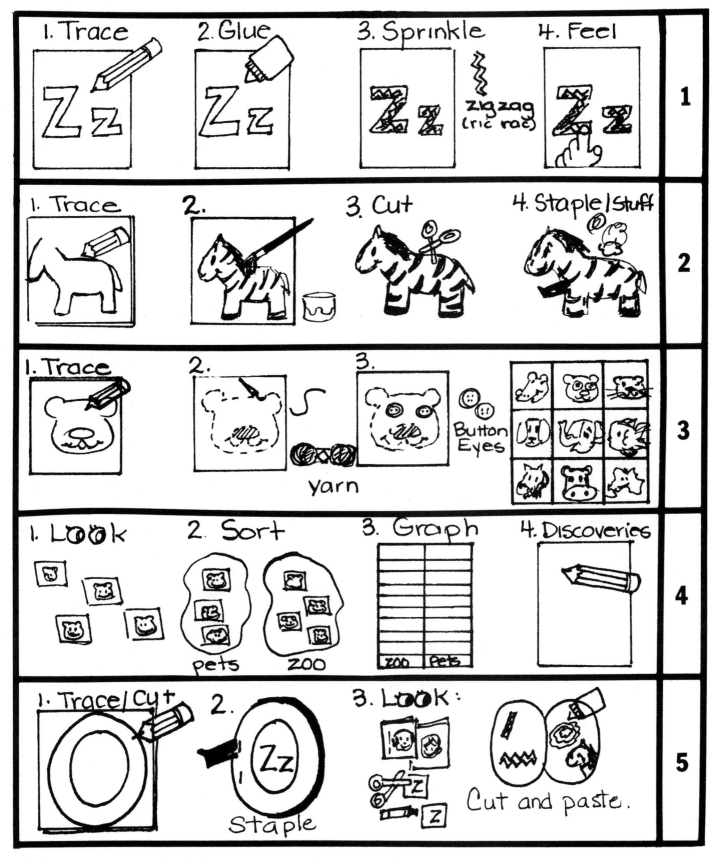

1

1. Trace   2. Glue   3. Sprinkle   4. Feel

zigzag (ric rac)

2

1. Trace   2.   3. Cut   4. Staple/Stuff

3

1. Trace   2.   3.   Button Eyes

yarn

4

1. Look   2. Sort   3. Graph   4. Discoveries

pets   zoo

zoo   pets

5

1. Trace/Cut   2.   3. Look:

Staple   Cut and paste.

CONTRACT MATERIALS and PROCEDURES:

1 9″×12″ construction paper for each child, glue, pencils, "Zz" tagboard letter patterns, ric rac (zigzags) to paste on.

2 Stuffed Zebra
Each child traces a large tagboard zebra pattern on two pieces of white butcher paper. One (or two) side of the pattern is outlined in black paint and decorated as a zebra. When dry, the zebra is cut out and stapled half-way around on the edges. Each is stuffed with crumbled newspaper then stapled shut.

3 Zoo Stitchery Hanging
Each child is responsible for one letter of the alphabet. Using free hand or a coloring book, each child traces the head of an animal depicting their sound on a burlap square 8″×8″. Burlap squares may be precut and stitched around the outside to prevent fraying . Using a running stitch, children stitch the outline of the animal with yarn. Buttons may be added for eyes. A parent volunteer stitches the squares together to make a hanging.

4 Sorting Zoo Animals
Provide several pictures each of zoo animal or "pet." Children sort the pictures (or plastic figures) into the sorting loops. Results are then graphed on the graph and discovery worksheet.

5 Zero Books
Children trace a pattern of a "zero" on 2 pieces of construction paper 9″×12″. The edge is stapled to make a book. Pictures of "Zz" sounds are pasted or drawn inside the book.

More Z Activities

SOUND OBJECTS:
 zigzag, zipper, zebra, zero, zinnia, zoo animals

SPECIAL INTERVIEW:
 Invite someone who has been to Africa to show his animal slides.

SPECIAL FIELD TRIP: to the zoo!

SPECIAL ANIMAL: zebra

SPECIAL DISCUSSION: zinc

TALKING TIME:
 If you could be any zoo animal, which would you choose to be?
 Which zoo animal are you most like? Why?

VOCABULARY: zinnia, zone, zeppelin, zinc

SCIENCE DISCUSSION: zeppelin
 How does it move?

SPECIAL ANIMAL: bee (makes ''z-z-z sound)
 Discuss hive, pollen, queen bee.

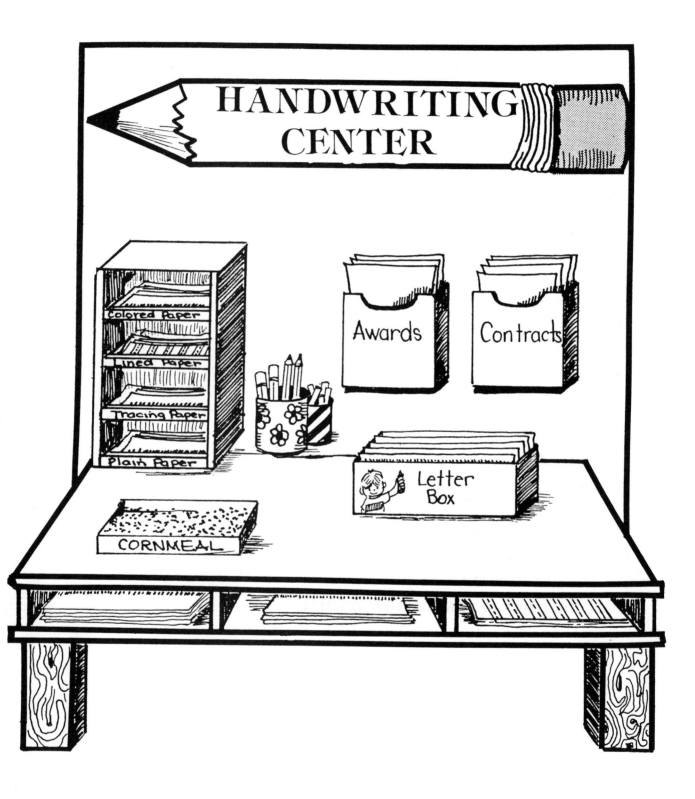

Materials

Handwriting Center

To help children practice writing each new letter sound they have learned, a handwriting center may be set up in the room. The Handwriting Time Contract contains many activities which may be used by individual children or groups of children to practice writing each new letter. Materials you may wish to provide at the center are:

1. Pipecleaners for forming letters
2. Clay to form letters
3. Precut burlap squares, yarn and large needles to make a stitchery letter
4. A box lid filled with sand or cornmeal for children to form letters
5. Paint, paint brushes and paper to paint letters
6. A small chalkboard, chalk and erasers to practice writing letters
7. Small blocks to build letters
8. A long jump rope to form letter shapes
9. Pencil and paper to practice letter printing
10. Crayons and paper to make large scribble animal letter drawings
11. "Feely Letters" made on cardboard squares. Form each letter shape with white glue. When it dries it will make a raised formation to the touch. These letters may be kept at the center.
12. A Handwriting Time Contract for each child

HANDWRITING TIME

Name

Make the letters with pipe cleaners.	Build the letter shapes with blocks.
Take turns tracing letters on each other's back.	Hop out the letter shape.
Make a letter stitchery.	Make the letters with clay.
Feel the letters blindfolded. What are they?	Jump out the letter shape.
Write the letters in the sand.	Trace the letter.
Paint the letters.	Crawl out the letter shape.
Write your letters on a chalkboard.	Make the letter into an animal.

Letter Express

Aa Bb Cc Dd

Students can make cars for a Letter Express

Ee Ff Gg Hh Ii

from ½ pint milk cartons!

Jj Kk Ll Mm Nn Oo

They'll enjoy filling the cars with small objects

Pp Qq Rr Ss Tt Uu

to match the sounds!

Vv Ww Xx Yy Zz

103

A Poetry Sound List

POETRY LIST

Poetry, Mother Goose and fairy tales provide a rich storehouse of images to provide the echolocation needed for letter sound knowledge. Sounds will echo back from the images. The list provided is but a sample. The anthologies used are: Ferris, Helen, *Favorite Poems Old and New*. Doubleday....Sheldon, William, *The Reading of Poetry*. Allyn and Bacon....Austin, Mary and Mills, Queenie, *The Sounds of Poetry*. Allyn and Bacon.

Sound Type	Poems	Source
Soft	*Fog*, Sandburg	Ferris
	Velvet Shoes, Wylie	Ferris
Loud	*Song Of The Train*, McCord	Ferris
	The Night Wind, Field	Ferris
Cutting	*The Bells*, Poe	Ferris
	Little Black Bug, Brown	Ferris
Colored	*I'll Tell You How The Sun Rose*, Dickenson	Sheldon
	In Praise Of Dust, Field	Sheldon
	Autumn, Smith *Blue Smoke*, Frost	Sheldon
	Things To Learn About, Becker Clothes, Frost	Sheldon
Slippery	*Primer Lesson*, Sandburg	Sheldon
	Night Things Are Soft And Loud, Gray	Sheldon
Smelly	*The Skunk*, Noyes	Sheldon
	A Boy's Summer Camp, Dunbar	Sheldon
	Smells, Worth	Sheldon
Tasty	*Peas*, Author Unknown	Sheldon
	Maple Feast, Frost	Sheldon
Letter Names	*P's The Proud Policeman*, McGinley	Austin-Mills
	C's The Circus, B's The Bus	Austin-Mills
Pictures	*On A Windy Day*, Gay	Sheldon
	Song Of The Train, McCord	Ferris
	Pictures In The Fire, Strong	Sheldon
	Cradle Song Of The Elephant, del Valle	Sheldon

"Can you think of anything else that begins with the same sound as fog that is as soft as the walk of cat's feet?" (fur, fuzz, foam)

"Draw a picture to illustrate the sound of silence and begins with the same sound." (smoke, sun, smile, sand)

"Draw a picture to illustrate something as soft as the noise of a cloud." (a feather falling, a butterfly flying)

"Listen, tell me who was really bad." (The children will love repeating the loud Yoooooooo!)

"I am thinking of something that makes a loud noise. It flies and begins with the same sound that you hear in Jack "(jet).

"Draw a picture that makes one of the sounds of a bell - give the beginning sound." (drum-dull bong, whistle-shart, cow moo-dull, brook-tinkle)

"What ends with the same sound as bug?" (rug)

"Draw a picture of an insect that makes a cutting sound." (bee-bzzzzzzzz, an old mouse squeak - eak, eak, eak, eak)

Fuse color with music. Play *The Rhapsody In Blue* and then have the children draw a thing that has a colored sound. (birds, waves, thunder, trees)

Read Dickenson's poem and ask what thing best showed the sun's color. (ribbon)

What is another color of the sun that begins with the same sound as ribbon? (red)

"List three things that have proud sounds that are not easy to call back because they walk away from you." (Read Sandburg's poem)

Fuse smell sounds with music. Play *The Grand Canyon Suite*. "What can you smell from the pictures you see?" (the sage, the dust cloud of the donkey's trot) (Worth poem) "Can you think of a poem that begins with the same smell sound made by Mr. Toad?" (P-Hew! - pot, pan, pie)

Read *"Peas."* "What made the peas stay on the knife?" (honey) "What has the same beginning sound?" (hat, house)

Read *"P's The Proud Policeman."* "Draw a picture of a thing that begins with the same sound as policeman." (pencil, paper, penny)

Read *"On A Windy Day."* Play *"Dance Of The Sugar Plum Fairies"* to fuse sound with the images created. "Draw a picture that brings back a sound in the poem." (leaves - dancing, trees -wave, thistledown - twirl)

Read *"Song Of The Train."* "What picture sound came from the train?" (click-ety-clack) "Can you name something that begins with the same letter sound?" (cat, cow, camel, canary)

Name_____

Date_____

I Know All My Letter Sounds

a b c d e
f g h i j
k l m n o p
q r s t u
v w x y z

The Growing Family of Good GOOD GA APPLE *Apple Products and Services Includes:*

4 Periodicals to Meet the Needs of Educators

THE GOOD APPLE NEWSPAPER Here's a year's supply of creative, easy-to-use ideas for your classroom. Each issue contains 16 BIG (17 1/2" x 22 1/2") pages and is filled with a limitless supply of ideas for all areas of the curriculum. Designed to provide you with a wealth of valuable materials. Packed with seasonal activities, arts and crafts, contests, bulletin boards and unique units of study—all designed by teachers. For teachers grades 2-8.

LOLLIPOPS Help make those early developmental years LEARNING YEARS with Good Apple's #1 resource for early childhood education. Provides timely teaching tips that will make your classroom come alive and articles that help to create a successful environment. Enjoy eye-catching bulletin boards, cut-and-paste activities, craft projects, songs, finger plays, gameboards, calendars and more. For preschool-grade 2 teachers.

CHALLENGE **Challenge** yourself and your students to inspiring interviews, thought-provoking games and activities, complete units of study and pages from our 20-page reproducible section. This wealth of articles, interviews, activities and units with special emphasis on art, music, drama, literature and the sciences will provide a special **Challenge** for your gifted students. For teachers and parents of gifted children preschool-grade 8.

OASIS Thousands of teachers are continuing to choose **Oasis** as their middle school classroom resource. Isn't it refreshing to know there's an **Oasis** of new and exciting ideas especially for middle grade teachers! It features interdisciplinary units, 2 full-color posters, current articles of interest, calendars, biographies, etc. For middle grade teachers 5-9.

Good Apple Idea and Activity Books

In all subject areas for all grade levels, preschool-grade 8+. Idea books, activity books, bulletin board books, units of instruction, reading, creativity, readiness, gameboards, science, math, social studies, responsibility education, self-concept, gifted, seasonal ideas, arts/crafts, poetry, language arts and teacher helpers.

Activity Posters • Note Pads • Software • Videos

and there is still more!

Good Apple is also proud to distribute Monday Morning books. This fine line of educational products includes creativity, arts and crafts, reading, language arts and early learning resources.

If a school supply store is not available in your area, please write for a FREE catalog to GOOD APPLE, 1204 Buchanan St., Box 299, Carthage, IL 62321-0299.